WRITINGS FROM
ANCIENT ISRAEL

WRITINGS FROM ANCIENT ISRAEL

*A Handbook of Historical
and Religious Documents*

Klaas A. D. Smelik

Translated by G. I. Davies

Westminster/John Knox Press
Louisville, Kentucky

First published 1991

PRINTED IN GREAT BRITAIN
9 8 7 6 5 4 3 2 1

Library of Congress Catalog Card Number 91-66030

ISBN 0-664-25308-3

CONTENTS

84999

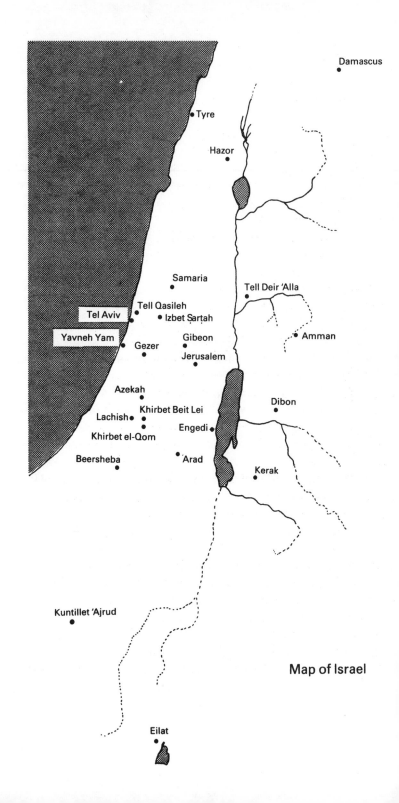

Damascus

• Tyre

Hazor
•

Samaria
•

Tell Deir 'Alla
•

Tell Qasileh
Tel Aviv •   • Izbet Sartah
Yavneh Yam   Amman
•

Gezer   Gibeon
•   •
Jerusalem
•

Azekah
•

Khirbet Beit Lei
Lachish •
•   Dibon
Engedi   •
Khirbet el-Qom   •

Beersheba   • Arad
•   Kerak
•

Kuntillet 'Ajrud
•

Map of Israel

Eilat
•

PREFACE

In Israel and Jordan many archaeological discoveries have been made, which throw new light on the Bible and the history of ancient Israel. Among these discoveries there are also inscribed potsherds, texts on stone, papyrus or plaster, seals and seal-impressions. A number of these texts are of little interest, but others deserve the attention of everyone who is interested in the Bible.

It is, however, not so simple to track these texts down. A few well-known ones, it is true, can be seen in illustrations in almost every book about the Bible, but most are known only to specialists. There are a few handbooks available, but these are – except for one – rather technical, and that one synthesis that was directed at a wider public appeared in 1958. Since then much has changed: the number of texts discovered has greatly increased and the interpretation of older discoveries has been improved at some points – reason enough for me to write this book.

Whenever one undertakes to write a guide of this kind, two possibilities are open. One can lay the emphasis on epigraphy, the correct decipherment of the letters and their philological interpretation. One would then propose new readings for obscure passages or new translations for unfamiliar Hebrew words. One can, alternatively, lay the emphasis on the historical significance of these discoveries of texts. It is the latter course that I have chosen.

Because of the large number of discoveries which have been made, particularly since the Second World War, it is impossible to deal with all the texts in this book. I have had to be selective. This was chiefly related to space and time. Only discoveries which have been made in the territory of the present states of Israel and Jordan have been included in this book and then only those from the period 1000–500 B.C.E., the time of the Israelite kings. To prove this rule the attentive reader will be able to point out a few exceptions which are in fact to be found in this book. In addition, I have not dealt with some texts which provide so little information that they would have tried the patience of the reader overmuch.

Anyone who goes deeply into Hebrew epigraphy will speedily observe that scarcely any text is translated by the experts in a single way. At times the proposals that are made are so remarkable that I could discount them completely. But often several possibilities remain open. I have considered whether I should quote alternative translations at the bottom of the page. But this did not seem a good idea to me. Therefore one translation of the texts is always given, in which words or phrases whose interpretation is uncertain are printed in italics. In a single case an alternative translation is given in the explanation with the text, but for the sake of readability I have been very restrained in this regard.

The translation itself is as literal as possible: even the Hebrew word-order is retained where it can be. Sometimes words are supplied, which do not stand in the original text but are necessary for the translation to be intelligible. These stand within round brackets. The original texts are often damaged or difficult to read. Lacunae or words which can no longer be deciphered are represented in the translation by three dots. Where it was possible to reconstruct with some certainty what must have stood in the lacuna, these restorations were indicated by square brackets.

A difficulty exists with the vocalisation of names. In these texts vowels are at best shown indirectly. From a technical point of view one should give the consonants alone, but that would have resulted in a rather unattractive appearance.

Therefore not QRḤH but Qarcho appears in the translation of the Mesha stele, even though this is possibly not the original pronunciation. Where possible the spelling used for biblical names in modern English versions of the Bible is adopted. The name of God is always rendered as YHWH, since I wish to adhere to the tradition of not pronouncing the name but replacing it, e.g., with the expression 'the Lord'.

At the back will be found a fairly comprehensive bibliography, which, however, offers more of a limited selection from the many articles and books which have appeared on this subject. Drawings of the texts discovered and sketch maps are an aid to my account. It was not possible to print the texts in the original language, but I refer those who are interested to the editions which are included in the bibliography.

J. van Dorp and E. A. Hemelrijk were so kind as to read critically through my manuscript, with the result that I was able to add a little more to the text here and there. I was glad to receive further suggestions for the improvement of the text from Dr. C. H. J. de Geus, Dr. A. Meinhold and Dr. H. Weippert. I would also like to thank my colleagues in the Institute Library of the Faculty of Theology in Utrecht and in the Bibliotheca Rosenthaliana at Amsterdam for their assistance, and especially Dr. G. I. Davies for his translation, which contradicts the Italian saying 'Traduttore traditore'. For the English edition the text has been revised at several points, and some new discoveries have been included.

I dedicate this book to the memory of my mother, the writer of children's books Jenny Smelik-Kiggen, who passed on to me her enjoyment of writing.

Chapter 1

INTRODUCTION

How does a writer become popular?

A surprising question with which to begin a book about discoveries of texts from ancient Israel. Yet a connection exists between it and the subject of this book.

If a writer wants to be widely read, it is not enough for him to be able to write well. There are so many other factors which play a part: the choice of subject, the fashion of the time, originality, personality, but sometimes also simply luck. This is true not only for writers of fiction: it also applies to a certain extent to scholars. One scholar is much more influential than another, without there being any difference in ability between them.

One sees this also with texts from the ancient world. The writings of the Syriac church fathers have, relatively speaking, received less attention from scholars, probably because Syriac is less familiar than Latin or Greek, not because the contents of these works are less interesting. There are dozens of texts originating from the ancient Near East which have not even been published yet, let alone been thoroughly studied. Texts on clay tablets, on sherds (*ostraca*), on papyrus or other writing-materials lie waiting in museum store-rooms. Now certainly the contents of the majority of these documents will not be world-shaking, but even among these texts interesting discoveries are made from time to time.

On the other hand, every discovery of a text from Israel and Jordan is greeted with the greatest possible attention, even though one must sometimes wait a long while before the text is at last published definitively. Texts which, taken by themselves, are not particularly fascinating have triggered off a stream of articles in the scholarly journals. The tip of the iceberg can be found in the bibliography at the back, which still amounts to some twenty pages. Illustrations of these texts can be found in every picture-book about the Bible or about Israel. In short, they are unusually popular, and that is not primarily due to their contents. Where, then, does this popularity come from? It comes from the fact that the Bible is such a popular book and they shed light on the cultural milieu in which the Bible, in particular the Old Testament, originated.

Firstly, it can be deduced from these texts, of which the most important are to be discussed in this book, that the use of writing among the Israelites only got well under way in the 8th century B.C.E. From the preceding period hardly any discoveries have been made. This could be the result of chance, the more so as papyrus – a widely used writing-material – does not stand up to the climate for long in most parts of Israel. But in Israel archaeological research is so far advanced that, whenever certain things are not or only rarely found, this also indicates that they did not exist, or only rarely existed, at that time there.

Therefore, it looks as if writing was indeed introduced among the Israelites in the time of King David (about 1000 B.C.E.), but initially only in royal court and government circles. A change from this comes about only in the 8th century. This relatively late extension of writing has consequences for the dating of biblical books (see further, chapter 2).

Secondly, the textual discoveries give additional information about the development of the Hebrew language, the meanings of words, proper names and idiom. A fine example of this concerns the translation of 1 Samuel 13:21. In the Revised Version this passage was still translated as follows:

> Yet they had a file for the mattocks, and for the coulters, and for
> the forks, and for the axes; and to set the goads.

A rather enigmatic statement. When weights were found in the 1930s inscribed with the term PYM, one of the words which occur in this verse that until then had not been understood, the verse at once became clear. PYM was a term for two-thirds of a shekel! As a result there stands in the Revised Standard Version of 1952:

> And the charge was a pim for the ploughshares and for the
> mattocks, and a third of a shekel for sharpening the axes and for
> setting the goads.

Thirdly, these discoveries of texts supply new data for the course of the history of ancient Israel. The most telling example of this is without doubt formed by the stele of Mesha of Moab, to which the third chapter is devoted. But the history of the last years of the kingdom of Judah also becomes notably more concrete through discoveries of texts, as will be evident from chapters 7 to 9.

The fourth point on which the discoveries provide us with valuable information concerns social and economic life in Israel during the Old Testament period. Inscribed potsherds (*ostraca*) report the delivery of goods and give indications of how the land was divided up at that time (see chapter 4). We also know more through these discoveries about administration, government and the organisation of the army (see, e.g., chapter 10). One discovery will especially appeal to the reader: this concerns a plea in favour of a poor farmer, whose cloak had been confiscated (see chapter 7).

Fifthly, the discoveries enlighten us about the religious situation in ancient Israel. What the Old Testament reports about this is strongly coloured by the prophetic viewpoint of the authors. We now possess some first-hand evidence of the religious practices of the Israelites which are condemned in the Old Testament (see chapter 11). Also notable is the discovery of a non-Israelite text, in which prophecies of the seer Balaam, who is known from the Old Testament, are recorded. Through this text the prophetic books of the Old Testament have been brought out of their literary isolation (see chapter 6).

In the sixth place, from outside the period with which this book deals, biblical manuscripts have been found. These are the famous Dead Sea Scrolls from the last two centuries before and the 1st century after the turn of the era. Our knowledge about the transmission of the books of the Old Testament has greatly increased as a result of this discovery. It would naturally be very significant if manuscripts from an earlier period were ever found, but, unfortunately, the chance of that is not great.

There are yet further areas of biblical research to mention, for which discoveries of texts have supplied new data, but this summary seems long enough to me to convince the reader of the importance of Hebrew epigraphy (the study of inscriptions). In what follows the emphasis will lie not so much on the linguistic aspects of Hebrew epigraphy but on the information which these texts offer for the interpretation of the Old Testament and for the reconstruction of the history of Israel in the time of the kings.

Writing

We live in a time which is not sparing in its use of writing. All around us we see letters, advertisements, slogans, newspapers, magazines and books. Even on cardboard milk cartons there is nowadays one thing after another to read. Apart from a small minority, everyone in the Western world can read and those who cannot often encounter difficulties – our society is not designed for the illiterate.

It is, therefore, difficult to imagine how life must be in a society where writing is lacking. Before five thousand years ago this was in fact the case throughout the world: writing had not yet been 'invented' – as you might say. But even after then writing was only in limited use. So in ancient Israel significantly less was written than in a modern country. There was less reading too, and when it was done it was done aloud. That means that, whenever we now read the Bible silently to ourselves with the same haste as we read the newspaper, we miss a lot. The Bible was not intended for that kind of consumption. One must read the text aloud and listen for the clever play on words and meanings that the writers offer to us, having counted on their work being recited aloud.

The great revolution which the development of writing brought about in human history has often been written about before. More interesting for this book are some other questions for investigation: How did writing begin? What kinds of writing were used in Palestine (I use the term in its strict geographical meaning for the region of the present-day states of Israel and Jordan)? What sort of writing-materials were used? Thanks to the research of the past hundred years answers to these questions can be given, but this becomes a somewhat complicated story that requires a certain amount of stamina. Those who do not possess this can move on to chapter 2.

How did writing begin? In excavations spread over a wide area in the ancient Near East small objects made of clay have been found, above all in storerooms. These objects, mostly not larger than 0.5–2.5 cm., are usually encountered in a number together and as far as their form is concerned they display little variation. So one can distinguish between twenty and thirty types. That makes it likely that they were symbols for a limited number of terms, for example numerals. One presumes that these clay symbols were placed in a jar or a bag (cf. 1 Samuel 25:29), to establish the number of objects or animals that one had entrusted to someone. Whenever a shepherd, for example, was given twenty-five sheep to look after, one put the clay symbols for twenty-five sheep in his bag or jar. When he brought the animals back again, the number could then be checked. On the basis of the finds it is thought that this system of administration was already in use around 8500 B.C.E.

In the fourth millennium B.C.E. life became more complex. Towns appeared; people followed more and more varied occupations (occupational differentiation) and a developed system of production and distribution of goods arose. In these circumstances more precise registration and administration than was previously usual came to be needed. Hence the types of clay symbols were changed to make it possible to hold more detailed information, and a system was also devised to prevent interference with the clay symbols. For it is clear that it cannot have been difficult for clay symbols to be removed from or put into the receptacle, whichever fraudulent intent required.

The solution to this problem which was chosen in the second half of the fourth millennium B.C.E. was the introduction of a new type of receptacle: a clay envelope in which the clay symbols were placed and which was then closed. On the outside the persons concerned rolled their cylinder-seals – an impression of a cylinder-seal functioned in Mesopotamia in the same way as a signature does today. Once it had been dried it was no longer possible for the clay envelope to be opened without this leaving visible traces. These clay envelopes could also serve as delivery notes: those who carried the consignment were given a filled clay envelope. On delivery it could be checked whether the number and type of the goods received corresponded to the clay symbols in the envelope, which was then broken. Anyone who delivered a consignment with a broken clay envelope could be sure that he would get into trouble.

This system worked well, but it was impractical, since between the sending and receipt of the shipment it was impossible to see how many clay symbols were in the envelope, and of what kind, without having to break it open. Why not, then, have the number and type of the clay symbols also indicated on the outside of the envelope? So it was done. Once this innovation had been introduced, the necessity for continuing to put clay symbols in the envelope became steadily less obvious. This practice was abandoned, and the typical form of the clay tablet came into being (around 3200 B.C.E.).

After this first phase in which only very simple communications were possible, these rudiments of a script developed in a comparatively short time, in Sumer, into the extensive and complicated system of the Mesopotamian script, with which in principle any piece of text can be written down. This script was from then on used not only for purposes of trade, but also with all the functions for which we use writing. From the ultimate form which the signs took the Mesopotamian writing system is called 'cuneiform' (wedge-writing).

The invention of writing did not, however, mean that all peoples began to make use of it immediately. This was a slow process of development: even in our own times writing-systems are being devised for peoples who have no experience of writing. Nor did it mean that every culture from then on came to use the same script. The first people that took over the principle of writing from the Sumerians, namely the Egyptians, already developed a form of writing of their own, namely hieroglyphic writing.

In Syria-Palestine Mesopotamian cuneiform was taken over in the second half of the third millennium and the second millennium (roughly 2300–1300 B.C.E.) for the writing of texts. In so doing the most accessible Mesopotamian language of the time was often also taken over as a written language, even though one spoke a different language oneself. In the city of Ebla (now Tell Mardikh), where important excavations were carried out by the Italians and an extensive archive was rediscovered, documents were written, for example, in Sumerian and in cuneiform, though there are also texts which are written in Eblaite, the local language of this city, which is a Semitic language comparable to Hebrew. For these texts in Eblaite cuneiform was also used.

More examples can be quoted: thus at Megiddo an Akkadian fragment of the famous Gilgamesh Epic in cuneiform was found, dating from about 1400 B.C.E. The most significant are the letters which the Canaanite city-rulers sent to the Pharaoh in Egypt in cuneiform and in a (degenerate) form of Akkadian. Akkadian, the language which was spoken in Babylonia and Assyria, is in contrast to Sumerian also a Semitic language, but of a different type from the languages which were spoken at that time in Syria-Palestine. Around 1500 B.C.E. Akkadian had become the language of diplomacy in the ancient Near East, which was even used by the Egyptian royal court for foreign correspondence. The scribes of the city-rulers of Syria-Palestine were well able to manage with the cuneiform script but had some trouble with Akkadian as a language. For this reason they sometimes moved over to their Canaanite dialect in their letters.

We know this above all from the discovery of the diplomatic archive of the Egyptian pharaohs Amenophis III and Amenophis IV – the latter better known by his later name Akhenaten – which was found in Akhenaten's capital Akhetaten (el-Amarna), that is, in Egypt. This archive from the 14th century B.C.E., uncovered in 1887, includes just under four hundred letters in Akkadian, most of them drafted by scribes from (south) Syria-Palestine. These documents show how the city-rulers of this region which stood officially under Egyptian authority had become involved in a continuing struggle for power. Many place-names which also occur in the Bible can be found in these letters. Perhaps the most striking among the rulers is Abdu-Kheba, the ruler of Jerusalem, who was so slandered by his opponents before the pharaoh that he judged the wiser course to be to write a letter to the Egyptian king. To this he added a P.S., with the request to the scribe who would read the letter to the pharaoh to do it with passion.

Here is this letter in translation:

Speak to my lord the king, Thus (speaks) Abdu-Kheba your servant. At the two feet of my lord the king I fall down seven times and seven times more. What have I done to my lord the king? I am slandered before my lord the king: 'Abdu-Kheba has become a rebel against his lord the king.' (But) see, it was not my father or my mother who set me in this place – the strong arm of the king has brought me into the house of my father. Why should I commit an offence against my lord the king? So long as my lord the king lives, I will tell the representatives of my lord the king: 'Why do you favour the Khapiru* and rebuff the city-rulers?' For that I am being slandered before my lord the king. And it is stated (by me): 'The territory of my lord the king is lost.' For that I am being slandered before my lord the king. Let my lord the king know: Now that my lord the king has put in garrison troops, Yankhamu (*the chief representative of the pharaoh*) has taken . . . There are no garrison troops. May the king take care of his land! The whole region has become rebellious against my lord the king. Ili-milku (*the ruler of Gezer*) is leading the whole of the king's land to ruin. May my lord the king take care of his land! I say (every time): 'I want to enter the presence of my lord the king and may I see the two eyes of my lord the king!' But the hostility towards me is strong and I cannot come into the presence of my

---

* The Khapiru are a group which are often encountered in the texts from this period, whose name recalls that of the Hebrews. They probably formed not a separate people, but an armed group which lived on the edge of society.

9

king. May the king think it right to send me garrison troops, so that I can come in and see the two eyes of my lord the king! So long as my lord the king lives, shall I say, as soon as a representative arrives (from Egypt): 'The territory of the king is lost. You do not listen to me. All the city-rulers are lost. The king has no city-rulers any more.' Let the king turn his attention to the archers, so that the archers of my lord the king sally forth! The king has no territory (any more), the Khapiru plunder the whole territory of the king. If there are yet archers this year, the territory of my lord the king will remain in being. But if there are no archers, the territory of my lord the king is lost.

(P.S.) To the scribe of my lord the king. Thus Abdu-Kheba your servant. Declare before my lord the king eloquently: 'The whole territory of my lord the king is lost.'

[Translated by Th. J. H. Krispijn]

The alphabet

Besides the use of Mesopotamian cuneiform, there was also experimentation in Syria-Palestine with various forms of writing, inspired by the Egyptian or Mesopotamian system. At different places short texts have been discovered, written with various signs for letters, whose significance we do not yet know for certain. The best-known texts were found in the Sinai peninsula and are in a script which is called Proto-Sinaitic, but the discoveries of texts from Gezer, Lachish and Shechem are still older (17th-16th centuries B.C.E.). It is thought that here we are already dealing with antecedents of the later Phoenician alphabet, and the script is spoken of as Proto-Canaanite.

A script that was inspired by the Mesopotamian system is the script (whose decipherment is certain) which was developed at the port of Ugarit (today Ras Shamra in northern Syria) in the 15th century B.C.E. and in which literary and other texts in Ugaritic (a Semitic language related to Hebrew) were written. The twenty-nine or thirty signs of the Ugaritic alphabet are similar in their form to the signs of the cuneiform script. In other respects, however, it is an entirely distinctive system, an alphabet in which one distinctive sign is used for each consonant (though in some cases vowels are also indicated). In comparison to Mesopotamian cuneiform this script is a great simplification and improvement.

Writing systems like cuneiform and hieroglyphs always required a lengthy training at a scribal school, before one was initiated into the complex and often inconsistent structure of the script and was able to write without help. Therefore knowledge of writing remained restricted to the small group which came into consideration for such training. An alphabetical system requires only a small number of signs (Hebrew, for example, has twenty-two), which each have a practically unambiguous sound-value. To acquire mastery of this script took much less time than was necessary for the learning of the then existing writing-systems. With this one of the conditions was created for a wider extension of writing into the different levels of society. But this must not be exaggerated. The adoption of the alphabet did not lead to everyone immediately being able to read and write. It took centuries before the population of Palestine was to some extent literate.

Although the Ugaritic alphabet was also used in Palestine in the 13th and 12th centuries B.C.E., it did not last. The Proto-Canaanite script won the day.

The end result (for the time being) of this process can be seen on the lid of the sarcophagus of king Ahiram of Byblos (c.1000 B.C.E.). The inscription displays a handy writing-system, the Phoenician alphabet. The text can be translated as follows:

> Sarcophagus which [Itto]baal (*vowels uncertain*), the son of Ahiram, the king of Byblos, made for Ahiram his father, when he interred him for ever. If now a king among the kings or a governor among the governors or the commander of a military camp has marched (against) Byblos and uncovered this sarcophagus, then

may the branch of his dominion lose its leaves, then may the seat of his kingdom be overthrown and then may peace depart from Byblos! As for him – may his inscription be erased. . . !

With the twenty-two signs which are not difficult to learn each writer can represent any word imaginable in Phoenician. Vowels were at first not indicated, but that is less of a problem for a Semitic language than, for example, an Indo-European language like English. Each sign was given a name: the first 'aleph', the second 'beth' (hence 'alphabet') and there was also a fixed order for the signs, so that they could be more easily learned and remembered. There is probably a connection between the name of the sign and its form. The first sign, 'aleph', represents an ox's head; 'aleph' also signifies 'ox'. The last sign, 'taw', represents a brand; 'taw' signifies 'mark'. Such a connection is not equally apparent in the case of all the other signs. The genius of the Phoenician alphabet is not this connection between name, form and sound-value of the sign, for the Sumerians had already thought of that. Rather it was that for the sign 'beth' one read not 'beth' but 'b', that is the principle that the first sound of the name alone constitutes the sound-value. In this way twenty-two signs could suffice, whereas a syllabic script, for example, requires at least eighty signs and a pictorial script many hundreds. This principle is called the *acrophonic* principle.

To begin with, the Phoenician alphabet was also used in Palestine. Thus the Gezer calendar (see chapter 2) is written in the Phoenician script. In the 9th century B.C.E., however, local variations arose, which developed into the palaeo-Hebrew and Aramaic scripts. The Greek alphabet too was derived from the Phoenician. The oldest text in a typical palaeo-Hebrew script is, surprisingly, the Moabite inscription of king Mesha of Moab (chapter 3).

The Phoenician alphabet as it appears on the sarcophagus of Ahiram has a form which makes it especially suitable for carving in stone with a stylus. It is consequently called *lapidary* ('lapis' is Latin for 'stone'). The palaeo-Hebrew script is, however, not lapidary, but *cursive*: that means more suitable for writing with a pen and ink on papyrus, leather or a potsherd (ostracon). Even when making a text on stone, for example, or a stone seal, in Israel a cursive script was used. This is probably an indication that the Israelite scribes rarely used stone as a writing-material, otherwise they would certainly have developed a lapidary script as well. That is consistent with the small number of discoveries of inscriptions on stone in Israel.

Now one might imagine that the script which is used today in Israel and in which the Hebrew Bible is printed is the same as the palaeo-Hebrew script of which we have spoken up to this point. But that is not the case. What we now know as the Hebrew script (often called 'square script' after the square shape of the letters) is in fact a continuation of the Aramaic script, not of the palaeo-Hebrew script. Anyone who sees the two writing-systems side-by-side will be even more struck by the differences than by the similarities (see fig. 1).

A remarkable course of events, but one that is historically intelligible. When the region of the Aramaean city-states (Syria) came under the political influence of the Assyrian empire (northern Iraq), the Assyrians began to be affected by cultural influence from the Aramaeans. It has often happened in history that the conqueror takes over the culture of the conquered (in part). A part of this cultural influence concerns the Aramaic language and script.

The Aramaic script offered great advantages over cuneiform and Aramaic is a language that could be understood by many non-Aramaean peoples of the Near East, with some effort. So it was Aramaic and not Assyrian which became the common language for the ever-growing Assyrian empire and this remained the case even when Assyrian rule collapsed.

Palaeo-Hebrew script	Square script	Modern cursive script	Transcription		Numerical value
𐤀	א	*k*	ʾālef	ʾ	1
𐤁	ב	*ǝ*	bēṯ	b, ḇ	2
𐤂	ג	*ċ*	gímel	g, ḡ	3
𐤃	ד	*ǝ*	dāleṯ	d, ḏ	4
𐤄	ה	*ą*	hē	h	5
𐤅	ו	*l*	wāw	w	6
𐤆	ז	*ƶ*	záyin	z	7
𐤇	ח	*n*	ḥēṯ	ḥ	8
𐤈	ט	*6*	ṭēṯ	ṭ	9
𐤉	י	*'*	yōḏ	y	10
𐤊	כ, ך	*ק, כ*	kaf	k, ḵ	20
𐤋	ל	*ſ*	lāmeḏ	l	30
𐤌	מ, ם	*Ɔ, N*	mēm	m	40
𐤍	נ, ן	*/, ⅃*	nūn	n	50
𐤎	ס	*o*	sāmeḵ	s	60
𐤏	ע	*ծ*	ʿáyin	ʿ	70
𐤐	פ, ף	*ℰ, ə*	pē	p, f	80
𐤑	צ, ץ	*ℰ, ℨ*	ṣāḏē	ṣ	90
𐤒	ק	*ק*	qōf	q (ḳ)	100
𐤓	ר	*ɔ*	rēš	r	200
𐤔	שׂ	*ė*	śīn	ś	300
	שׁ	*ė*	šīn	š	
𐤕	ת	*Ω*	tāw	t, ṯ	400

Fig. 1 Palaeo-Hebrew and the Square Script (adapted from Nat-Lettinga, *Grammatica van het Bijbels Hebreeuws)*

Aramaic remained the language of diplomacy and officialdom. Thus in Saqqara a letter has been found from a ruler in Palestine to the Pharaoh of Egypt, from about 600 B.C.E., written in Aramaic (see chapter 9). Only in the Hellenistic period (after Alexander the Great) was Aramaic gradually displaced as the official language by Greek.

When Aramaic came to serve as an official language, the Jews too began to adopt Aramaic as a spoken language. The Jewish community in Elephantine in Egypt used Imperial Aramaic as a written language (5th century B.C.E.), but even in the land of Israel itself Aramaic came to be both written and spoken. In the time of Jesus the situation had even reached the point that Hebrew continued to serve as the spoken language of only a small number of Jews in the neighbourhood of Jerusalem, and it otherwise continued to be used only by the learned. Most Jews spoke Aramaic or Greek. In the New Testament, as a result, a few Aramaic words are quoted in the text which is otherwise in Greek, such as 'abba', 'maranatha', 'talitha qum' and 'mammon'.

On the other hand the change from the palaeo-Hebrew to the Aramaic script should not be regarded as absolute. The original palaeo-Hebrew script remained in use for a long time after the Aramaic script had been introduced. It was used for biblical manuscripts, inscriptions and legends on coins: still on the coins which were struck during the two Jewish revolts (66–73 and 132–135 C.E.) there are words in the palaeo-Hebrew script. There is an interesting phenomenon in some of the manuscripts from the Qumran caves, where the whole (Hebrew) biblical text is reproduced in Aramaic square script, except that for the divine name the palaeo-Hebrew script is preferred. After 135 C.E. the palaeo-Hebrew script ceased to be used by the Jews, but a development from it, the Samaritan script, is favoured to this day by the Samaritan community in Israel.

Writing materials

As a third and final point: what writing materials were used? It has already been noted that in Israel few inscriptions on stone have been discovered. This applies also to texts on metal, though at Qumran a copper scroll was discovered with an interesting account on it of where some treasure was hidden and recently two tiny silver scrolls were found in Jerusalem (see chapter 11). Mostly pottery, leather, wood and papyrus were used, and later parchment (leather after preparation) as well. Because of the unfavourable climatic conditions most of this has been lost. Only around the Dead Sea have leather and papyrus survived.

Other writing materials were also used: writing-boards covered with wax, plaster (see chapter 6), (precious) stones – for signet rings and weights; in the Roman and Byzantine periods texts were even formed from mosaic cubes. What is surprising is the absence of clay tablets as a writing material, the more so because clay tablets in cuneiform have in fact been found in Palestine. This results from the fact that the Phoenician script and its successors take a form which makes them less suited to clay tablets. Outside Israel there is one case of a short note in Aramaic being inscribed on a clay tablet, but in Palestine that did not happen.

While an iron stylus was used for writing on stone (cf. Jeremiah 17:1; Job 19:24), a person who was going to write on an ostracon, or leather or papyrus, would take a pen and ink. A scribe also had a wooden palette (Ezekiel 9:2, 3, 11), with a compartment for his pens and deeper cavities for the ink (black and, sometimes, red), and a penknife (Jeremiah 36:23) with which he could cut off a leaf from a papyrus roll or sharpen his pen.

In the communal building of the Jewish sect which lived by the Dead Sea and from which the Dead Sea scrolls derive, a special room was set apart for the work of writing. The excavators came upon plastered writing tables and even ink-wells. Here some of the Dead Sea scrolls were probably written. In this later period the copying of Hebrew biblical manuscripts developed into a special craft associated with its own ritual. Very precise rules concerning this are set down in one of the so-called minor tractates of the Babylonian Talmud, called *Soferim* (which means 'Scribes'). And still today the Torah scrolls which are to be used in synagogue worship are copied by hand according to these regulations. In this respect scarcely anything has changed over two thousand years.

Chapter 2

TWO MONTHS – INGATHERING
THE GEZER CALENDAR

What is then the oldest surviving Israelite inscription? Is it the so-called agricultural calendar from Gezer, or is it the potsherd (*ostracon*) from ʿIzbet Ṣarṭah, which was found in Israel in 1976? Or is it neither of the two?

In the previous chapter it has already been noted that in Palestine the Phoenician script was originally used, and that only in the 9th century B.C.E. did local variants emerge which developed into distinct types of script. That means to say that with discoveries older than the 9th century it is impossible to say on the basis of the script whether we are dealing with an Israelite inscription or not.

Is this really so essential? Are we not dealing here with a question of the same order as the dispute over whether the local pride of my home town of Haarlem, Larens Janszoon Koster, rather than that German impostor Gutenberg invented the art of printing? That would be a wrong impression to give, for in fact the issue here is concerned with the problem of when the Israelites themselves started to write. And an answer to this question is in turn of great importance for the dating of the documents which the authors of the Old Testament used, when they wrote about Israel's past. For these (written) documents cannot be older than the introduction of writing among the Israelites.

If one could make the data in the Old Testament one's starting-point, already Moses had the ability to write and in the time of the Judges an ordinary youth from Succoth could write out the names of the seventy-seven rulers and elders of the place for Gideon (Judges 8:14). These biblical passages are, however, difficult to bring into harmony with the epigraphic data – the texts discovered in this area which date from earlier than the 8th century B.C.E. are very few in number.

It is certainly dangerous in archaeology to use an argument based on the absence of certain finds (*argumentum e silentio*): for new discoveries could be made which would change the whole picture. In the present case, however, this is not to be expected. Israel has been, from an archaeological point of view, very thoroughly investigated and the overall picture shows that writing was only used in Israel on any substantial scale after 800 B.C.E. Moreover, the famous 19th-century scholar Julius Wellhausen had already reached this conclusion on the basis of data in the Old Testament alone. The prophecies of Elijah were not made into a book of the Bible, while those of Isaiah were, since – so Wellhausen observed – in his time it was usual to record things in writing, whereas in Elijah's time this was not yet so.

This difference between a number of passages in the Bible and the archaeological data is, however, less important than perhaps it seems. The passages mentioned derive from parts of the Hebrew Bible whose authors did not have the intention of writing history like a modern historian. They themselves lived in a later period, when writing was quite widespread and they did not worry about the question whether this had also been the case in the earlier periods which they described. If it was useful in their narrative for someone to write, then they let him write – anachronism or not.

To assume, on the basis of these passages in the Bible, the spread of writing among the Israelites before 800 B.C.E. is thus also unjustified from a methodological point of view. One is then using Scripture for a purpose for which it was not intended.

However, it is possible to deduce from the Old Testament

that in the time of King David scribes were in use at the court (cf. 2 Samuel 8:17 and 20:25). Their names are given respectively as Seraiah and Sheia or Sheva: the second name is probably Egyptian and suggests that this scribe was not an Israelite by birth. That is also to be expected: outside Israel scribes were a regular part of the personnel in the king's service. When David introduced a royal court into Israel, he also took over this institution of court scribe from his foreign models. A reader might perhaps wonder why we are quite ready to take these data from Scripture as historical but not, for example, the story of the youth from Succoth. That is because the passages in which David's court scribes are mentioned must be derived from old annals. This can be seen from the style of these passages, whereas the story in Judges is clearly a narrative which was drafted and written by the biblical author himself.

If scribes were in use at the court of David and Solomon, does this mean that Israelites outside the court also used writing or did this remain a preserve of the palace? For an answer to this question archaeological discoveries are of great importance. So we return to the ostracon from ʿIzbet Ṣarṭah and the agricultural calendar from Gezer.

The ostracon from ʿIzbet Ṣarṭah

In 1976, during the excavations at ʿIzbet Ṣarṭah, a village in the vicinity of Aphek which is identified by the excavator (without much reason) with biblical Ebenezer, two potsherds were found. They fitted together and had been inscribed. On this ostracon there are eighty-three letters, which do not make up a coherent text, though nearly the whole alphabet is found there, written from left to right. We have clearly to do with a writing exercise, not a text with a definite content. The discovery demonstrates that at ʿIzbet Ṣarṭah in the 12th

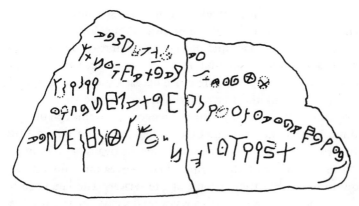

Fig. 2 Ostracon from ʿIzbet Ṣarṭah

century B.C.E. someone made the attempt to learn how to write. But was this person an Israelite? According to the excavator, M. Kochavi, this question is to be answered in the affirmative. The potsherds were discovered in a silo belonging to a house, which according to him was occupied by Israelites, in view of the ground-plan and the pottery. Now such identifications are very risky: according to other archaeologists one cannot just assume that these types of house and pottery were used exclusively by Israelites, so that it is far from certain that this sherd was really inscribed by an Israelite, and not for example by a Canaanite.

The Gezer Calendar

Likewise with the Gezer calendar: it is impossible to say with certainty whether it was a Canaanite or rather an Israelite who wrote it. The script and dating leave both possibilities open. The dating of this discovery is, moreover, a problem in itself. The Gezer calendar was found in 1908 by R. A. S. Macalister during his devastation masquerading as an excavation of the archaeological remains at Tell Jezer, biblical Gezer.

Macalister's method of excavation was so inexact that he could only report that the limestone tablet (only 6.7–7.2 × 11.1 cm in size) was found in a layer which extended from the 11th to the 6th century B.C.E. One cannot get very far with that kind of dating: it is therefore necessary to date the tablet on the basis of the form of the letters. Since the text was probably drawn up by an inexperienced hand, this can only be done with some caution. One comes then to a date a little before 900 B.C.E., i.e. a time soon after the death of Solomon.

On the basis of the script, then, we cannot answer the question of the ethnic origin of the writer. The language in which the text is written also gives no decisive answer on this. Reference has been made, it is true, to some letters which were added in the margin of the text, which some would like to interpret as 'BY. It has been proposed to read these as Abijah,

Fig. 3   Calendar from Gezer

a proper name which is typically Israelite. In that case the tablet could certainly be regarded as Israelite. The letters 'BY could, however, also stand for *'ābî*, 'my father', while at Ugarit a proper name Abiya occurs. In addition, the possibility exists to interpret the three letters not as 'BY but as 'BG (aleph, beth, gimel). Then the writer simply started to write out the Phoenician alphabet, but did not complete it. In brief, what is written in the margin does not provide any certainty either.

If we must leave open the question whether the Gezer calendar is the oldest Israelite inscription, the inscription itself is interesting enough. This calendar can be translated as follows, though one should take into account that there is still no agreement among the experts about certain details of the interpretation:

> Two months: ingathering. Two months:
> sowing. Two months: *late grass.*
> One month cutting of flax.
> One month barley harvest.
> One month harvesting and measuring.
> Two months: pruning (vines).
> One month summer-fruit.

The first question which this inscription raises is: to what months do these descriptions correspond? For the usual names for the months are missing from the inscription. On the basis of the way in which farming was carried on in Palestine in the last century, it is possible to form a reasonably good picture of farming in the biblical period, because the methods used only changed to a limited extent in between. Only in the present century has this changed. With this information it is possible to give an answer to the question.

The calendar begins with two months' 'ingathering', meaning the harvest of the summer fruit, grapes and olives, which lasts approximately from August to November. The calendar thus begins in the autumn, just as today the Jewish New Year also falls in September. The Old Testament also knows of a New Year which falls in the spring – hence the present-day Jewish New Year falls on the first day of the *seventh* month (cf. Leviticus 23:24).

The writer of the Gezer calendar in any case presupposed a year that began in August/September – that is why he does not begin his calendar with the month in which sowing is done – which would have been more logical seen from an agricultural point of view.

After the two months' 'ingathering' – we are here dealing with lunar months of twenty-nine or thirty days – come two months for sowing. The early rains fell then – sowing was continued until January (or even February). Then follow two months 'late grass'. In the original the word is LQŠ, a word that occurs in Amos 7:1 and is there translated in the RSV 'the latter growth'. There is, however, not complete agreement over whether this word here signifies a late sowing or grass that grows during the late rains which fall before the harvest begins (March–April). With the reckoning of this calendar there is a certain difficulty with the second alternative – according to the inscription LQŠ should fall in January–February. Hence the suggestion to translate not 'late grass' but 'late sowing'.

The following month is set apart for the cutting of flax. The expression 'cutting' is surprising in this connection because it was usual to pull flax out of the ground, not to cut it. The solution to this problem is probably the following: it is here not a matter of harvesting of flax to make clothes from it but of collecting the seeds which can serve as food or from which oil can be pressed. For these purposes flax is indeed cut.

After the flax harvest the barley has the next place, and only after that comes the wheat. This sequence also appears in Exodus 9:31–32 in a parenthesis during the story of the plagues in Egypt: 'And the flax and the barley were beaten down, for the barley was in the ear, and the flax was in bloom. But the wheat and the spelt were not beaten down, for they come later.'

The ninth month in his calendar is designated by the writer as 'harvesting and measuring'. By harvest he means the wheat harvest – the most important harvest in the year, which is completed in mid-June. 'Measuring' – the translation is not completely certain – refers to the measuring out of the grain on the threshing-floor, a very important event, not only for the farmer, who can now see how big a harvest he has gathered, but also for the creditors and the officials who came to collect the tax in kind.

The following two months are characterised as the time of pruning (of vine-tendrils). This is remarkable, considering that one should preferably not prune in summer, unless a second pruning is meant, to facilitate the grape harvest in the coming months. The last line speaks of summer-fruit, by which figs, pomegranates and such like are meant.

Writing exercises

Now that we have gone through the text with its peculiarities, the question of what the author's aim was in writing this inscription (which is now in the Archaeological Museum in Istanbul) will have to be raised. In this connection the fact that the tablet must have already been used before – traces of earlier letters can still faintly be seen – gives an indication of the direction in which we must look, namely in the direction of the world of ancient oriental scribal schools. On the basis also of the unusual form of the tablet, which makes it easy to hold in the hand and able to be hung up, it may be supposed that it functioned as a kind of slate.

The use of writing makes special instruction necessary.

While prehistoric man taught his children himself the skills which were necessary to stay alive, children in Egypt and Mesopotamia had to be instructed in the art of writing by teachers. From both the regions mentioned texts have been handed down which make it possible to form for oneself a reasonably detailed picture of the methods of teaching. For just as even now one finds reading exercises in school books, by which children – as if it is not bad enough just to be in school – are also treated to subjects like 'Peter at school', in antiquity too school life was considered an especially suitable subject for reading matter.

One of the favourite topics for this was punishment and how to avoid it. In these schools it was certainly no gentle affair, as this scarcely child-friendly statement bears witness: 'The ears of the pupil are on his back'. This quotation comes from an Egyptian writing-exercise. A Sumerian text is somewhat more subtle. In this the pupil is advised, whenever he is on uncertain terms with his teacher, to get him invited home and well entertained by his father. For a few suitable presents and kindnesses can quickly bring a disturbed relationship between teacher and pupil back to normal again.

But not only life at school, but also other subjects came up for consideration. In Mesopotamia there was a great predilection for lists of words and names, arranged topically. In this way one learned not only how to write but also the names of trees, animals, towns, countries, stones and minerals. In Egyptian writing exercises one is struck above all by the large number of cautionary tales. Alongside this, the pupils practised by writing out model letters or amusing parodies of them. This last type allowed them an occasional laugh amid the beatings with the cane and the sermons about morals.

When it is seen against this background, it is natural to suppose that the Gezer calendar too was a writing exercise, for which an enumeration of the activities of a farmer is chosen as a generally educative subject. The charming stories which have been told about this calendar – a simple farmer's boy writing down on this tablet the activities which took place through the year on his farm – are thus misplaced. The writer of the Gezer calendar was probably not destined to be a farmer but a scribe.

A scribe at that time occupied a role which can best be compared to that of a modern civil servant. For up and coming officials it was certainly not without value to know what, among other things, farmers were doing in the fields. Then they could choose the right point in time to collect the taxes, which were then taken in kind. Precisely in the 10th century B.C.E. an organised system of taxation and compulsory labour came into operation in Israel. A farmer's son learned in a quite different way how the land must be farmed: he worked on it from an early age with his father.

The Gezer calendar thus stands in a line with the ostracon from 'Izbet Ṣarṭah – both are evidence of instruction in writing, as this must have taken place in ancient Canaan, but about which only a little is known – in contrast to Egypt and Mesopotamia. They are the forerunners of later writing exercises, which this time were discovered in a clearly Israelite context and which can be dated to the second half of the monarchy period. These texts, chiefly written on ostraca, but

Fig. 4. Lion scratched on a staircase of the fortress at Lachish. Right: letters in ancient Hebrew script, among others the first five letters of the alphabet (Lemaire, *Les Écoles*, p. 13).

also for example on a step of a staircase, consist mostly of a number of letters in alphabetical order, sometimes filled up with drawings – like those which children still do today (and adults during meetings). A nice example of this is reproduced here (see fig. 4).

Such writing exercises have been discovered at Lachish, Kadesh Barnea and Kuntillet Ajrud, among other places. Through these discoveries we do get some idea of the teaching of writing in ancient Israel, a subject on which the Hebrew Bible is surprisingly silent.

Chapter 3

KEMOSH WAS ANGRY WITH HIS LAND:
THE MESHA STELE

In the course of time the river Arnon (now known as Wadi el-Mojib) has cut itself a deep valley in the Jordan plateau. Travellers who followed the King's Highway, the great north-south route in Transjordan, descended the steep slope by a zig-zag track only to climb up again hundreds of metres in the same fashion, on the other side of the river. It is still the same today, though asphalt covers the old road.

Just to the north of this natural barrier lies the village of Dhiban, a name which recalls that of biblical Dibon, the capital of King Mesha of Moab. Right outside the modern settlement lies the ancient mound which has been identified with Dibon. Remains of stone walls are still clearly discernible, but what one sees is not from the time of Mesha (9th century B.C.E.), but from a later period. From the city of King Mesha little was found during the various archaeological campaigns which have been undertaken here by the Americans since the Second World War. Even so King Mesha has become famous as a result of an archaeological discovery.

The Moabites

It may be assumed that the Moabites were closely related to the Israelites. Their language differs little from Hebrew and their strong sense of a bond with their national god Kemosh is reminiscent of ancient Israelite religion. The name Moab appears for the first time in Egyptian texts from the time of the famous pharaoh Ramesses II. During the tumultuous events around the transition from the 13th to the 12th century

B.C.E., when groups from the Aegean region who were called 'Sea Peoples' by the Egyptians completely disrupted the unsteady equilibrium in Western Asia, the Moabites saw their opportunity to bring an area permanently under their control. In the same way the Edomites, Ammonites and Israelites are also recognizable as new peoples at exactly this time. The territory of the Moabites lay principally between the Arnon and the 'brook' Zered, which is now known as Wadi el-Hasa. 'Brook' is too modest a term; the river-valley of Wadi el-Hasa is even more impressive than that of Wadi el-Mojib.

The expansion of the Moabites was, however, directed northwards. This brought them unavoidably into conflict with the Israelites, who considered a part of the region north of the Arnon as their rightful heritage. The depth of the hatred between the two peoples is evident from the many prophecies against Moab which one comes upon in the Old Testament (Isaiah 15–16; 25:10–12; Jeremiah 48:1–47; Ezekiel 25:8–11; Amos 2:1–3; Zephaniah 2:8–11). It is also evident from the ban on admitting Moabites into the congregation of YHWH (Deuteronomy 23:3; cf. Nehemiah 13:1), though according to Ruth 4:22 none other than King David was of partly Moabite ancestry.

The antipathy which the Israelites bore towards their neighbours becomes clearest when one reads the story about Lot and his daughters (Genesis 19:30–38). For although it is admitted in this story that the Israelites and Moabites were related to one another through Lot, the latter prove to have an ancestor who was conceived in very dubious circumstances indeed. The support which the Moabites, as appears from 2 Kings 24:2, gave to the Babylonians when their armies ravaged Judah in 598 B.C.E., cannot be far from the origin of this insulting story. If we are looking for historical evidence, we should do better to leave this text, like the stories about the battle with King Sihon of Heshbon (Numbers 21:21–30) and the coming of Balaam (Numbers 22–24: see further below, chapter 6), out of consideration. The story about the Moabite king Eglon too (Judges 3:12–30) does not yet bring us to historical fact. One might well begin with the subjection of the Moabites to Israel in the time of David. After Solomon died about 927 B.C.E. (on the dates of the Israelite kings there is no agreement among scholars) and his kingdom split into two parts, the tide was to turn for the Moabites and they recovered their independence, though further details are lacking.

The discovery

In 1868 an Alsatian missionary from Jerusalem, whose name was Klein, was shown by his Arab guide at Dibon a black basalt stone measuring 1.15 m. high and 60–68 cm. across. On it stood an inscription which, Klein was assured, no one had yet been able to decipher. Even though it was by now dark and he had no time to study the text properly, he realized at once that he was dealing with an important discovery and he notified the Prussian consul. He showed interest, but the English and French, who had heard about the stele, also made efforts to obtain the stone. Such great interest in a stone appeared suspicious to the local population and they came to the conclusion that in the stone they must have something special in their possession. The stone was heated, cold water was poured over it and through the sudden cooling the stone broke into pieces. If they had expected to find a treasure, they came away disappointed, but the pieces could serve well as amulets in granaries – the special power of the stone was a guarantee of that.

This very important text would have thus been all but lost, were it not for the fact that an ambitious young Frenchman, Charles Clermont-Ganneau, had already had squeezes made of the stone. Moreover he managed to get possession of about

Fig. 5 The Mesha stele

two-thirds of the original stone, albeit in fragments. The pieces were directed by way of Jerusalem to the Louvre in Paris, where the stone was put together again and the gaps filled on the basis of the squeezes (see fig. 5). For all that the inscription has somewhat suffered (above all at the end). But for the most part it can be read without much trouble. Here is a translation of it:

I am Mesha, the son of Kemosh[-yatti], the king of Moab, the Dibonite. My father was king over Moab for thirty years, and I was king after my father.

And I made this high-place for Kemosh in Qarcho . . . because he has delivered me from all *kings*, and because he has made me look down on all my enemies.

Omri was the king of Israel, and he oppressed Moab for many days, for Kemosh was angry with his land. And his son succeeded him, and he said – he too – I will oppress Moab! In my days did he say [so], but I looked down on him and on his house, and Israel has gone to ruin, yes, it has gone to ruin for ever!

And Omri had taken possession of the whole la[n]d of Medeba, and he lived there (in) his days and half the days of his son, forty years, but Kemosh [resto]red it in my days. And I built Baal Meon, and I made in it a water reservoir, and I built Qiryaten.

And the men of Gad lived in the land of Atarot from ancient times, and the king of Israel built Atarot for himself, and I fought against the city and captured it, and I killed all the people [from] the city as a *sacrifice* for Kemosh and for Moab, and I brought back the fire-hearth of his *uncle* from there, and I hauled it before the face of Kemosh in Qeriot, and I made the men of Sharon live there, as well as the men of Maharit.

And Kemosh said to me: Go, take Nebo from Israel. And I went in the night and I fought against it from the break of dawn until noon, and I took it and I killed [its] whole population, seven thousand *male citizens and aliens, and female citizens and aliens*, and servant girls; for I had put it to the ban for Ashtar Kemosh. And from there I took th[e ves]sels of YHWH, and I hauled them before the face of Kemosh.

And the king of Israel had built Jahaz, and he stayed there during his campaigns against me, and Kemosh drove him away before my face, and I took two hundred men of Moab, all its *division*, and I led it up to Jahaz. And I have taken it in order to add it to Dibon.

I have built Qarcho, the wall of the woods and the wall of the citadel, and I have built its gates, and I have built its towers, and I have built the house of the king, and I have made *the double reser[voir for the spr]ing* in the innermost part of the city. Now there was no cistern in the innermost part of the city, in Qarcho, and I said to all the people: Make, each one of you, a cistern in his house. And I *cut the moat* for Qarcho by means of prisoners from Israel.

I have built Aroer, and I made the military road in the Arnon. I have built Bet Bamot, for it was destroyed. I have built Bezer, for [it lay in] ruins.

[And the me]n of Dibon stood in battle-order, for all Dibon, they were in subjection. And I am the kin[g over] the hundreds in the towns, which I have added to the land.

And I have built [the House of Mede]ba and the House of Diblaten and the House of Baal Meon, and I brought there . . . flocks of the land.

And Hauranen, there lived . . . Kemosh said to me: Go down, fight against Hauranen! I went down . . . [and] Kemosh [resto]red it in my days . . . From there . . .

And I . . .

Two other inscriptions

Since then two more inscriptions have been discovered in this region, which possibly derive from Mesha. Unfortunately they are very fragmentary. The first of these was found at Dhiban in 1951. On the broken piece of stone it is still possible to read:

The house of Ke[mosh].

The second was found in 1958 at Kerak. Here it is a matter of a fragment of what was probably a statue with an inscription on it. In any case it is thought that the pleated hem of a robe can be recognised notwithstanding the fragmentary state of

Fig. 6 Moabite inscription from Kerak (from *ZDPV* 80 (1964), 170).

the artefact (see fig. 6). In this inscription the name of Kemosh-yat (or Kemosh-yatti), the father of Mesha, appears. That need not signify that we are dealing here with an inscription of the father of Mesha, since Kemosh-yat is of course also mentioned in the first line of the Mesha stele.

Possibly the text may be translated as follows:

> [I am Mesha, the son of Ke]mosh-Yat, the king of Moab, . . .
> . . . Kemosh for a fire-place, because . . .
> . . . and behold, I made . . .

Unfortunately not much more of this building-inscription can be made out.

For the inscriptions of Mesha characters were used which correspond to what was customary in Israel at the time. It is not improbable that Moab came under strong cultural influence from Israel and that scribes connected with the royal court of Israel were brought in. The language of the inscription is probably not Hebrew, but Moabite. This language, however, differs little from Hebrew. In this type of script, as already stated, vowels were not recorded, and so in the translations given above the representation of the vowels in names is uncertain. Where this was possible I have used the pronunciation known from translations of the Bible.

The writing is of a high quality and words and sentences are separated from one another by special signs, which makes interpretation easier. In the translation it was unfortunately not possible to show that in this inscription the personal pronoun 'I', which is rather rarely used in the Semitic languages, occurs surprisingly often, especially in the sections which deal with Mesha's building activities. That is where Mesha's great merit lies, according to the author. Where he is dealing with the war against Israel, however, the first person pronoun is singularly lacking. In this way the writer suggests that these achievements are more the work of Kemosh than of Mesha, who merely carried out the orders of his god.

Explanation of the text

At first glance the inscription on the Mesha stele looks for the most part like a boastful victory-report, in which the story is told of how the Israelites were brought to their knees. One may then be greatly surprised by the appearance of several disjointed statements about other important deeds of the king and by the lack of coherence in the text.

On a closer look, however, the text proves to hang together better. Moreover, it is important to realize that here we are not dealing with a victory-report, as was thought until recently, but with a building-inscription. Building-inscriptions are encountered all over the Near East. Their intention is to preserve the name of the building in remembrance, not only by men, but also by the gods, for they chiefly commemorate the building of a sanctuary. The original simple inscriptions, in which the builder stated his name and his building activity, developed in the course of time into extensive narratives of the great deeds of the king who had the sanctuary erected or restored. Evidently the opportunity to enumerate even more excellent deeds was too tempting for these rulers to let it pass by.

The Mesha stele too is such a building-inscription. In fact it is about the fact that he built 'this high place for Kemosh in Qarcho', but this declaration hardly stands out any more among the number of military achievements which Mesha boasts that he has achieved. This all comes across to us rather unsympathetically, but it was the custom at the time.

It was also the custom that the king began by introducing himself as a lawful ruler – Mesha does this by saying that his father before him was king of Moab. Mesha was thus no usurper, who had secured the throne for himself by force, but was descended from a royal family. Next he states why this stele was set up, namely to commemorate the building of a sanctuary in Qarcho (probably a new quarter of the capital Dibon). Such a sanctuary is referred to (just as is the case in the Old Testament) as a 'high place'. Probably the Mesha stele itself stood on the 'high place' to preserve the name of this king for ever in remembrance in the mind of the god Kemosh and of the Moabite people.

Mesha built this sanctuary after his great victory over his enemies because it was his conviction that it was the god Kemosh who had brought him his deliverance.

One of the most interesting aspects of this inscription is the fact that its world of ideas resembles so strongly that of the Old Testament. This passage is a clear example of this: just as the God of Israel is praised because he saved his people out of the hand of their enemies, so here Kemosh is glorified, since he saved Mesha from all his adversaries.

It is also according to custom that in this kind of text a description is inserted of the wretched circumstances in which the king began his rule. The more bankrupt the business that he inherited from his predecessor the greater his own achievement. When Mesha began to rule, Moab was oppressed by Israel; but now Israel is destroyed for ever. The latter is of course a gross exaggeration: in fact Mesha only succeeded in bringing to an end Moab's subjection to Israel and recovering the land of Medeba (see map, fig. 7). But such exaggeration is typical of the style of this kind of text, just as recently Iran and Iraq both at the same time claimed crushing victories over each other, before another war began.

After a short description of building activities at two places in this area around Medeba (Baal Meon and Qiryataim), there follows a trio of military victories (Atarot, Nebo and Jahaz). These were apparently the three most important strongholds of the king of Israel in this area, from which Moab was kept under control. The order in which the three places are mentioned is surprising, if one looks them up on the map. It does not seem very probable that this is the chronological order, since then Mesha would have followed a very dangerous strategy, seeing that Jahaz is the closest to Moab and so the king of Israel could easily have cut the supply lines of Mesha's troops.

The writer, who was in Mesha's service, devoted (relatively speaking) his greatest attention to the capture of these places. He also exhibits his talents here, for each capture is described in a different way. Particularly the battle for Nebo is described in a lively way which again strongly recalls the Old Testament. In 1 Samuel 15:3 God says:

> Now then, go and you shall defeat Amalek and you must put to the ban all that is his!

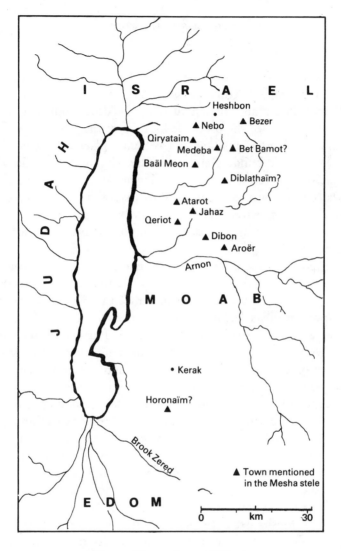

Fig. 7   The territory of Moab

In the Mesha stele Kemosh says the word:

Go, take Nebo from Israel.

Thereafter the writer concentrates on the building activities of Mesha: Qarcho, Aroer, the military road in the Arnon, Bet Bamot, Bezer, and the sanctuaries at Medeba, Diblataim, and Baal Meon – for the probable location of these places see fig. 7. When Mesha says that he has built a place, that generally means he did building and especially rebuilding there. It was chiefly a matter of military building activities. New defensive walls with towers and gates had to arise, and water-reservoirs had to be constructed – all this to resist a possible siege. Water-supply was a particularly important point in warfare, as will appear again in chapter 5.

A good infrastructure was of course also necessary to make it possible to move troops quickly. At the beginning of this chapter it was already indicated that the Arnon forms an important obstacle for through traffic; which is why Mesha had a military road constructed here. Further the damage done during the war had to be repaired and new settlers from other parts of Moab had to be moved into the area where the original Israelite populations had been slaughtered.

After this passage about Mesha's many building achievements comes another description of a military action, this time not in the region to the north, but to the south-west of Moab (at least if Hauranen is the same place as biblical Horonaim). Probably Hauranen was then an Edomite town, but the stele is here too badly damaged for the details of the account to be understood any longer. In the concluding part of the Mesha stele (which has not survived) there was probably a curse-formula directed at anyone who might damage the stele. History does not recount whether the inhabitants of Dhiban who caused the Mesha stele to shatter into fragments fell victim to the ancient curse of the king.

The role of Kemosh

It has already been indicated that the way in which the national god of Moab, Kemosh, is spoken of in this text is strongly reminiscent of the Old Testament. At first Kemosh was angry with his land, which gave Israel the possibility of oppressing Moab. But in the time of Mesha Kemosh's attitude changed: he directs the operations to increase the power of Moab. In thankfulness Mesha not only builds a sanctuary for Kemosh, but he also gives his conduct of war a ritual character. The captured spoil of Atarot and Nebo is hauled 'before the face of Kemosh', that means, is brought to his temple. In addition the Israelite population is slaughtered as a sacrifice to Kemosh.

Similar language is used in the Old Testament about the anger of YHWH, which leads to Israel being overwhelmed by enemies, and also about leaders who, with God's help, bring deliverance to the people and then the enemy population are slaughtered to make room for the people of God. The parallelism is striking. But at the same time it must be noted that in antiquity people generally took for granted that the gods were involved in wars between men. Anyone who knows the epics of Homer will agree with this. Conflict on earth means conflict also in the heavenly regions, where the national gods step into the arena with one another and then if necessary descend to the earth to settle the dispute. When a god is not strong enough, his people suffer defeat and they can raise a lament together.

Where, however, devotion to the deity is very strong the believer cannot accept that his (or her) deity might be weaker than the gods of other peoples. His (or her) god is so mighty, that he or she cannot suffer defeat. If victory is then not secured, this must be the result of the fact that the deity was so angry with his own people that help did not come. The deity must be placated, and then the victory should not be long delayed.

Ritual warfare

Although these ideas about the role of the deity in war were quite general in antiquity, it is the ancient Israelite view which resembles most clearly that which we encounter in the Mesha stele. That also applies to the mode of warfare. Although there were naturally also utilitarian reasons for the horrifying massacres which are reported, these are represented in the texts as attempts to quieten the anger of the deity or as the execution of his commands. They therefore have a ritual character, as already noted.

It is striking in this connection that Mesha puts the inhabitants of Nebo to the 'ban', since this ritual is also mentioned in the Old Testament (cf. Numbers 21:2f.; Joshua 10:28–40; Judges 1:17, 21:11; 1 Samuel 15:3; 1 Kings 20:42). It has indeed been wondered to what extent the ban was actually carried out by the Israelites. The Mesha stele may be an indication that the relevant biblical narratives and regulations do not merely derive from a fantasy about a 'holy war' but that in some cases the population of an enemy city in its entirety was in fact dedicated to the God of Israel in the sense of being killed. The seven thousand inhabitants of Nebo were in any case subjected to this cruel ritual, in honour of Ashtar Kemosh, a combination of the god Ashtar (the male equivalent of Ashtart (Ashtoreth)) and Kemosh.

The ban is not mentioned in the description of the slaughter at Atarot. Here the writer uses a different term which probably means 'sacrifice' – in any case here again it is a matter of a ritual. For a correct interpretation of the biblical passages in which such cruel rituals are mentioned it is important to keep in mind that such ritual warfare was also current outside Israel at the time.

It is interesting to read that, according to Mesha, the men of Gad lived 'from ancient times' in Atarot. This suggests that

Mesha was not acquainted with the biblical tradition that Gad had taken part in the Exodus from Egypt as one of the Israelite tribes. Is this the result of faulty knowledge on Mesha's part or was the tribe of Gad in fact not involved in the Exodus, but had always lived in Transjordan? An interesting problem that is closely connected with the whole question of the origin of the Israelites, but one that cannot be gone into more closely here.

The counter-attack of Jehoram

The Israelites did not meekly let Mesha's actions against them go unanswered, although one gets the impression from the Mesha stele that in the main they just let themselves be killed off.

In 2 Kings 3:6–27 we are told about a grandiose expedition which the Israelite king Jehoram (851–845) undertook together with his Judaean counterpart Jehoshaphat (868–847) and an unnamed king of Edom (which at this time had apparently regained its independence – cf. however 1 Kings 22:48!), to force Mesha back into subjection. Here is the narrative of Kings:

> Now Mesha king of Moab was a sheep breeder; and he had to deliver annually to the king of Israel a hundred thousand lambs, and the wool of a hundred thousand rams. But when Ahab died, the king of Moab rebelled against the king of Israel. So King Jehoram marched out of Samaria at that time and mustered all Israel. And he went and sent word to Jehoshaphat king of Judah, 'The King of Moab has rebelled against me; will you go with me to battle against Moab?' And he said, 'I will go; I am as you are, my people are as your people, my horses as your horses'. Then he said, 'By which way shall we march?' Jehoram answered, 'By the way of the wilderness of Edom.'
>
> So the king of Israel went with the king of Judah and the king of Edom. And when they had made a circuitous march of seven days there was no water for the army or for the beasts which followed

them. Then the king of Israel said, 'Alas! The Lord has called these three kings to give them into the hands of Moab.' And Jehoshaphat said, 'Is there no prophet of the Lord here, through whom we may inquire of the Lord?' Then one of the king of Israel's servants answered, 'Elisha the son of Shaphat is here, who poured water on the hands of Elijah.' And Jehoshaphat said, 'The word of the Lord is with him.' So the king of Israel and Jehoshaphat and the king of Edom went down with him.

And Elisha said to the king of Israel, 'What have I to do with you? Go to the prophets of your father and the prophets of your mother.' But the king of Israel said to him, 'No; it is the Lord who has called these three kings to give them into the hand of Moab.' And Elisha said, 'As the Lord of hosts lives, whom I serve, were it not that I have regard for Jehoshaphat the king of Judah, I would neither look at you, nor see you. But now bring me a minstrel.' And when the minstrel played, the power of the Lord came upon him. And he said, 'Thus says the Lord, "I will make this dry stream-bed full of pools." For thus says the Lord, "You shall not see wind or rain, but that stream-bed shall be filled with water, so that you shall drink, you, your cattle, and your beasts." This is a light thing in the sight of the Lord; he will also give the Moabites into your hand, and you shall conquer every fortified city, and every choice city, and shall fell every good tree, and stop up all springs of water, and ruin every good piece of land with stones.' The next morning, about the time of offering the sacrifice, behold, water came from the direction of Edom, till the country was filled with water.

When all the Moabites heard that the kings had come up to fight against them, all who were able to put on armour, from the youngest to the oldest, were called out, and were drawn up at the frontier. And when they rose early in the morning, and the sun shone upon the water, the Moabites saw the water opposite them as red as blood. And they said, 'This is blood; the kings have surely fought together, and slain one another. Now then, Moab, to the spoil!' But when they came to the camp of Israel, the Israelites rose and attacked the Moabites, till they fled before them; and they went forward, slaughtering the Moabites as they went. And they overthrew the cities, and on every good piece of land every man threw a stone, until it was covered; they stopped every spring of water and felled all the good trees; till only its stones were left in Kir-ḥareseth, and the slingers surrounded and conquered it. When the king of Moab saw that the battle was going against him, he took with him seven hundred swordsmen to break through, opposite the king of Edom; but they could not. Then he took his eldest son who was to reign in his stead, and offered him for a burnt offering upon the wall. And there came great wrath upon Israel; and they withdrew from him and returned to their own land. (2 Kings 3:4–27 [RSV])

Comparison of the texts

How then are the story in 2 Kings 3 and the account on the Mesha stele related to one another? Is it possible, on the basis of these two documents, to establish what in reality took place?

Both documents are not to be relied on without further consideration. Mesha's account is, as already noted, not organized in a chronological but in a systematic order. Moreover it displays the characteristics of this type of text as they appear everywhere: gross exaggeration, silence about anything unfavourable to the king (e.g. defeats), an exclusive interest in military and building activities. The text has of course the advantage that it derives from the time of the events themselves.

The period in which a text like 2 Kings 3 originated is a disputed matter. This chapter probably contains a historical core, but around that a story has been developed which has legendary and theological features. This applies especially to the appearance of the prophet Elisha. But this account is clearly less determined by the theological standpoint of the author than the parallel version in 2 Chronicles 20:1–30. Whoever reads that in the Bible will observe how in the retelling of the story from 2 Kings 3 in Chronicles the historical event is entirely relegated to the background.

The story in Chronicles concentrates on the pious king Jehoshaphat, and in the style of the stories in Joshua it is God himself who sees to the victory. The enemy destroy one another without a blow needing to be struck. For the Judaean troops there remains only the task of plundering the enemy camp. The point of the story is prophetic theology: God alone is the guarantor of his people's security. Consequently the account in 2 Chronicles 20 can from now on be left out of account when we are trying to reconstruct the historical course of events.

The inscription of Mesha begins with the fact that the Israelite king Omri (882–871) has subjugated Moab and annexed the land of Medeba to Israel, while the rest of Moab remains under its own rule. The land of Medeba comprises the area north of the Arnon, which according to the Old Testament belongs to Israel, but not according to Mesha. Besides it appears from the inscriptions of Mesha that the land immediately adjacent to the Arnon on the north side always remained in Moabite hands, even in the time of Omri: Dibon and Aroer did not need to be recaptured from Israel.

There is no reference to the subjugation of Moab by Omri in the Old Testament. If the books of Kings had been intended as history in the usual sense of the word, then this might be thought very surprising. But the books of Kings do not represent the past in a straightforward way: the theological viewpoint of the author is so determinative that this important political development is not reported, because Omri belongs to those kings who are judged unfavourably by the writers. Anyone who wishes to read about the valiant deeds of this king is referred to the Book of the Chronicles of the Kings of Israel, a writing that has not been preserved (cf. 1 Kings 16:27). Given the general prosperity of Israel in the time of Omri and Ahab, there is therefore no reason to doubt the historicity of the report of the subjugation of Moab by Omri.

But then it comes to a counter-stroke by Mesha. Kings is

explicit about this: when Ahab died, Mesha rebelled against the king of Israel (2 Kings 1:1, 3:5). If the death of Ahab is placed in 852, we come to 852 or 851 B.C.E. for the revolt. The Mesha stele is less informative in this respect. Mesha says nothing directly about a refusal to continue any longer in dependence on Israel. Was it too painful to report, because this rebellion must have involved the breaking of his oath as a vassal-ruler? For it was customary that when the vassal had a treaty imposed upon him he had to affirm this under oath: breach of the treaty then called down the wrath of the gods upon him. For that reason the vassal had also to swear by his own national god, to prevent the god from supporting him any more in battle (cf. Ezekiel 17:11–21).

Mesha does refer to the recovery of the land of Medeba by Moab forty years after Omri had taken possession of the land. With that we reach about 840. But before referring to the forty years, he states that Omri lived there in 'his days and half the days of his son.' Since Ahab, Omri's son, probably ruled from 871–852 we come to about 860, giving a discrepancy of twenty years.

Something does not fit: as a result different scholars have come up with their solutions and no solution is completely satisfactory. Now forty years is an indication of time which is so stereotyped that we do not need to take it literally. It could just as well have been thirty. But it is not very probable that Mesha would have succeeded in reconquering the land of Medeba in the time of Ahab, since Ahab had at his disposal an unusually strong army, as we know from Assyrian sources. Moreover Mesha cannot have occupied this region and at the same time remained a vassal of Israel. His revolt must therefore have taken place before the conquest of the land of Medeba, but according to Kings the revolt occurred only after Ahab's death, which is more probable than during Ahab's reign.

Some have wanted to understand 'his son' as a collective: 'his descendants' would be intended. The last descendant of Omri was killed in 845, so we come to 858. And that is still in the time of Ahab, and so too early. Moreover the Mesha stele seems to speak quite clearly about one person, who is referred to as Omri's 'son'. Consequently it is better to understand 'son' as 'descendant' (singular) and suppose that it here means the Israelite king Jehoram (Omri's grandson), who ruled from 851 to 845. Then we come to 848. The whole reign of Ahab was then, for convenience, left out by Mesha in his indication of the time as 'his days and half the days of his son'.

If this dating of the conquest of the land of Medeba is accepted, then the revolt of Mesha can be placed immediately after the death of Ahab. In the history of the ancient Near East one can find further examples of vassal-rulers rising in revolt after the death of a powerful suzerain. Mesha could then have refused, during the short-lived reign of Ahab's son Ahaziah (852–851), to continue paying tribute. Because of his illness (see 2 Kings 1) Ahaziah had no further opportunity to undertake any counter-measure to this. His brother and successor Jehoram did attempt it, and with that we come to the story in 2 Kings 3.

Yet it does not seem very probable that Jehoram set off immediately on this campaign which led through very inhospitable territory, with its unavoidable risks. He must first have campaigned in the north, in the land of Medeba. The Bible says nothing about this, but on the Mesha stele it is noted: 'And the king of Israel had built Jahaz, and he stayed there during his campaigns against me, and Kemosh drove him away before [my] face'. In my opinion this refers to King Jehoram, who was driven out from Jahaz. For Jahaz lies just to the north of Dibon and was one of Israel's southernmost strongholds in this region (next to Atarot). Apparently Jehoram tried, from this base, to force Mesha back into subjection, but his action was a failure. He had to retreat and Atarot, which he had fortified, also fell into Moabite hands. Afterwards Mesha captured Nebo.

When he had, in this way, obtained control of the land of Medeba, Mesha fortified a considerable number of towns in this region, so as to be in a position to withstand an attack from the north. Jehoram and Jehoshaphat, however, decided to surprise Mesha by making an attack from the south-west, even though it was a dangerous route, as is clear from the story in 2 Kings 3.

Thus they succeeded in forcing their way into Moab from the south to the north and confining the Moabite king within the fortified town of Kir-Hareseth (possibly Qarcho). A sally by Mesha in the direction of the king of Edom (whose loyalty towards Judah and Israel was probably dubious) failed, and apparently the king saw only one way out left: he sacrificed his first-born son on the wall of the besieged city where the Israelites would be able to have a good view of it. By bringing this sacrifice he probably hoped to appease Kemosh's anger and to make his luck turn in the battle. The text concludes unclearly: 'And there came great wrath upon Israel; and they withdrew from him and returned to their own land' (2 Kings 3:27). What precisely is meant here is not clear: who is angry? Kemosh? YHWH? Israel? In any case the writers of Kings acknowledge that Israel did not succeed at that time in subjugating Moab. It is unclear whether the action against Hauranen (Horonaim) which is mentioned in the Mesha stele still has something to do with the campaign of Jehoram from the south. Even less do we know how things went thereafter between Mesha and Jehoram. It looks as if Jehoram resigned himself to the fact that he could not defeat Mesha. It is even possible to suggest that it was only the Israelite retreat from Kir-Hareseth which made it possible for Mesha to conquer the territory to the north of Dibon. In that case the military actions mentioned in the earlier part of the Mesha inscription took place *after* the events alluded to in 2 Kings 3, and not before.

It should have become clear to the reader how important the Mesha stele is for the study of the Old Testament, as a historical source and as evidence of a religion which is closely related to that of Israel. This discovery is even so unique that several scholars have tried to show that it is a forgery which was commissioned by the Frenchman Clermont-Ganneau. In fact, for Old Testament research this discovery is almost too good to be true.

Chapter 4

IN THE TENTH YEAR
OSTRACA FROM SAMARIA

In the Bible we hear of one people Israel, which marches together to the Promised Land under the leadership of Moses and Joshua, to establish themselves there. In this the biblical authors are more presupposing an ideal than giving a faithful description of historical reality.

In the preceding chapters we have already often seen that the biblical authors were not historians in a modern sense. In fact the people Israel originated from the union of a number of different population groups, which in part, and probably even a large part, had already lived for centuries and centuries in the land of Canaan. From ancient times, Mesha even supposed (see above, p. 33). If we read through the relevant stories in the Old Testament attentively, the authors clearly intimate that in reality a sense of unity was hard to find among the Israelite tribes. They were aware that in their story of the conquest of the land they were describing an ideal situation, but they hoped that what had not been achieved in the past would indeed happen in the future; the recovery of independence for all Israelites in one land.

The different groups which ultimately developed into the people Israel did not occupy the whole land of Canaan. Other peoples were there too – in the Old Testament many names are mentioned (cf., e.g., Genesis 15:19–21) – who lived around, but also within, the areas occupied by the Israelites. In times of war it was therefore difficult for the Israelites to maintain mutual contact, because they had first to pass through hostile territory, before they could meet one another.

The weakest link was between Judah in the south and the

tribes to the north of Jerusalem, because this city – then inhabited by Jebusites – lay, as a foreign enclave, in between their respective territories. When the Israelites in the north recognised Saul as king, there was no automatic enthusiasm for this in Judah, although Saul is presented in the books of Samuel as ruling over Judah too. That want of enthusiasm is clear from the fact that, after Saul's death, they opted not for his son Ishbaal (Ishbosheth), but for Saul's adversary David. David was separately proclaimed king of Judah at Hebron and only later did he obtain the throne in the northern part of Israel. After capturing Jerusalem he established himself in this city: a new royal residence for a new united state.

David's grandson Rehoboam soon lost his grip on the unity of the kingdom: the Israelites in the north were no longer prepared to be governed from Jerusalem. The family of David was for them a representative of Judah and not a native ruling house. It was Jeroboam I who was able to co-ordinate these feelings of discontent into a regular revolt, which brought him to the throne of Israel. The kingdom fell apart into two sections: Judah in the south remained faithful to the dynasty of David, while the north went its own way, and this new kingdom (very confusingly) is also called Israel. For clarity we shall speak of 'the northern kingdom of Israel', while using 'Israel' as the general designation for the whole land or people.

While it was self-evident for the Judaeans that Jerusalem should remain the capital and royal residence – was this not where the temple and the royal palace were? – as far as the northern kingdom was concerned it was less clear which city should become the capital. There was a succession of experiments: Shechem, Penuel and Tirzah. But none of the three was satisfactory as a capital. In the case of Tirzah, the poor communications between the city and the rest of Israel and the limited extent of cultivable terrain were probably the reasons why the king who resided there looked for another residence.

A new capital

Omri, of whom we already spoke in chapter 3, came to power by means of a military coup, and he was determined to found a dynasty of his own, mightier than that of David. For this he needed a new capital. Just as David chose Jerusalem as a city in neutral territory (for Jerusalem was not in the territory of one of the Israelite tribes, but right between Judah and the North), so Omri founded his capital in a place which was at that time unoccupied. This avoided rivalry between the different urban centres in the northern kingdom and it put him in a position to build a city entirely according to his own design, unhindered by existing buildings. He bought the site from Shemer and named the city Samaria after him (at least according to 1 Kings 16:24).

The site was especially favourable for a city: the hill on which Samaria lay towers above its surroundings, which consist of fertile farmland, and an important route from north to south ran and runs past it. The city founded by Omri and enlarged by Ahab then remained the capital of the northern kingdom of Israel until the Assyrians captured Samaria in 722/1 B.C.E. The luxury of the inhabitants was even so great that the prophet Amos turned against it:

> Proclaim to the strongholds in Assyria,
> and to the strongholds in the land of Egypt,
> and say, 'Assemble yourselves upon the mountains of Samaria,
> and see the great tumults within her
> and the oppressors in her midst.'
> 'They do not know how to do right,' says the LORD,
> 'those who store up violence and robbery in their strongholds.'
> Therefore thus says the Lord GOD:
> 'An adversary shall surround the land,
> and bring down your defences from you,
> and your strongholds shall be plundered.'

Thus says the LORD:

'As the shepherd rescues from the mouth of the lion
two legs, or a piece of an ear,
so shall the people of Israel who dwell in Samaria be rescued,
with the corner of a couch and part of a bed.'

'Hear and testify against the house of Jacob,'
says the Lord GOD, the God of hosts,
'that on the day I punish Israel for his transgressions,
I will punish the altars of Bethel,
and the horns of the altar shall be cut off
and fall to the ground.
I will smite the winter house with the summer house;
and the houses of ivory shall perish,
and the great houses shall come to an end,' says the Lord.

(Amos 3:9–15 [RSV])

Its capture in 722/1 B.C.E. did not, moreover, mean the end of Samaria. It remained a capital, even if no longer of an independent state but of a province of the Assyrian empire. In the Persian period too, Samaria was the residence of the governor. In 322 B.C.E. the city was conquered by Alexander the Great and Samaria became a centre of Greek culture. In 108 B.C.E. John Hyrcanus, the Hasmonaean king, completely destroyed the city. However people continued to live in Samaria and in 30 B.C.E. the city came into the possession of Herod the Great, who rebuilt it and gave it a new name: Sebaste, in honour of Caesar Augustus (Sebastos is Greek for Augustus). This name of Sebaste lives on in the name of the modern village of Sebastiye.

The site of ancient Samaria was investigated archae-ologically by the Americans from 1908 till 1910 and later by a combined expedition of Americans, British and the Hebrew University of Jerusalem. The principal discovery was the royal palace precinct of Omri, later reconstructed by Ahab, which lay on the acropolis of Samaria. This is not the place to go into more detail about the excavation of Samaria. It can at least be mentioned that, in addition to the inscribed pot-sherds, which were found there and which will have a central place in this chapter, a fragment of a monumental Hebrew inscription was discovered, with only one word on it: '*asher*, the relative particle in Hebrew. It needs no demonstration how important it would have been if more of this inscription from the time of the Israelite kings had survived. In addition, there is a fragment of an inscription in cuneiform, probably from the time of Sargon II, the Assyrian king who was responsible for the destruction of Samaria in 722/1 B.C.E.

The ostraca

One of the buildings which was exposed in 1910 gave the impression of having been a storehouse. The building was situated between the palace of Omri and the western part of the casemate wall. Here, in two side-rooms, the American expedition from Harvard found the ostraca which have come to be known as the Samaria ostraca. In 1932 a further ostracon (no. C1101) was found, but its interpretation is so uncertain that we shall leave it out of consideration here.

Ostraca (singular: ostracon) are potsherds on which a text is written in ink or incised. Because pottery was at that time used for more purposes than today and it is (as is well known) easily broken, there were always potsherds available. Other writing-materials were expensive (papyrus) or more difficult to use (stone). As a result, for texts of only temporary value (notes, receipts, writing exercises, letters and memoranda) sherds were used. Most of the pottery from the area was quite light in colour on the outside during this period so that if dark ink was used the legibility was good.

In all 102 ostraca were found, of which some were incised but the majority written in ink. Many are easily legible, others

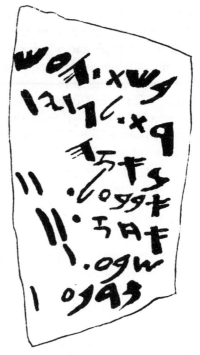

Fig. 8 Ostracon no. 2 from Samaria

less so, and there are some of which not a single word can be deciphered any more. The information on the ostraca is really not very exciting. For example, the text on ostracon 2 can be translated as follows:

> In the tenth year. For Gaddiyaw. From Azah. Abibaal 2. Ahaz 2. Sheba 1. Meribaal 1.

Although all these texts are short and very simple in structure, their interpretation turns out to be very difficult. So difficult, that there is even now no agreement about what these ostraca are about: is it a matter of accounts of tithes (taxes) which were delivered in kind to the palace and stored in this building? Have the ostraca a connection with the provisioning of the palace? Or are we dealing here with produce from the royal domains which is destined for courtiers?

If one compares what is written on the different ostraca, it is striking that the structure remains in principle very much the same, but that the fixed elements in them are not always present in the same combination. The elements are: the date, the type of produce (wine or oil), the name of a place or a district preceded by the Hebrew preposition *min*, and personal names which are sometimes preceded by the Hebrew preposition *le*. A simple text may offer, for example, only date and topographical indication and 'oil':

> In the tenth year, vineyard of Yehaweli, a jar of oil for washing. (no. 55).

No. 19 gives rather more:

> In the tenth year *mi(n)* Yazit, a jar of oil for washing, *le* Ahinoam.

Besides oil, wine can also be mentioned:

> In the ninth year *mi(n)* Quseh, *le* Gaddiyaw, a jar of old wine (no. 6).

The text can be more extensive:

> In year 15, *mi(n)* Shemyada, *le* Heles Gaddiyaw, Gerah Hannah (no. 30)

i.e. date, *min* and name of a district, *le* and personal name, (an) other personal name(s).

The meaning of *min* here is quite clear: it refers to the place from which the oil or wine originated. The places and districts named all lie in the vicinity of Samaria. But *le* is rather ambiguous: it can refer to the owner, or the person for whom the consignment is intended or the person to whom payment is made. This uncertainty is the reason why such divergent interpretations of the texts are possible.

The most probable of these interpretations seems to be the theory mentioned above in third place. An objection to the first theory (tax payment) is that the names of the officials to whom oil or wine is to be paid are not always the same for each district, but that two places from a single district are mentioned in connection with two different names. In addition there is sometimes a single name which is used in connection with different districts. The interpretation which argues that we are here dealing with the provisioning of the palace is also less probable: why so many names and why such small quantities?

Wine and oil for the courtiers

According to the third explanation, we are here dealing with the delivery of oil and wine, originating from the king's domains and intended for his courtiers. We have to imagine this in the following way. The king had surrounded himself with nobles, who lived in the capital. These exalted people were not in a position to provide for their own livelihood, nor could they take charge of an estate whose yield could feed them and their families, in view of the fact that they were required to remain with the king at court. Therefore overseers were necessary. The land was mainly the property of the king himself, but he was kind enough to assign the yield of certain estates to his faithful courtiers. The estate was managed by an overseer, and he had to hand over a part of the yield to the courtier to whom it was assigned. The receipts for these payments would then be represented by the ostraca which were found at Samaria: the personal name preceded by *le* is that of the courtier; the second name is that of the overseer.

Biblical texts can also be brought in to illustrate this

practice. In 1 Samuel 8 the prophet Samuel responds to the desire of the people, who demand a king so as to be like all other peoples, by sketching an extremely sombre picture of the activities of a king, which actually will not have differed much from the practice of the time. One of the measures which, according to this text, the king would take is that:

> He will take the best of your fields and vineyards and olive orchards and give them to his servants. He will take the tenth of your grain and of your vineyards and give it to his officers and to his servants. (1 Samuel 8:14–15)

This practice is also alluded to in 1 Samuel 22:7.

Still more details are provided in 2 Samuel 9. After all Saul's sons have died or been murdered, and David has no more competition to fear from that side, he decides to honour the lone survivor, a crippled son of Jonathan. Mephibosheth (originally Meribaal) is allowed from then on to eat regularly at David's table and has restored to him all the lands of Saul which had come into David's possession. Because Mephibosheth regularly ate at the king's table, he lived at Jerusalem and could therefore not manage his estate himself. Therefore David appointed Ziba, a servant of Saul, to work the land with his family and servants and gather in the harvest 'so that the son of your lord may have bread to eat' (2 Samuel 9:10). If one day a receipt should ever be discovered on an ostracon for the yield of this estate, its texts could possibly read like this (in translation): 'In year 15 from Benjamin for Mephibosheth, son of Saul, (from) Ziba, the servant of Saul, a jar of oil'. The story of Mephibosheth and Ziba has, moreover, a surprising sequel, as can be read in 2 Samuel 16:1–4 and 19:24–30.

Dating

On the basis of similarities in the script and the fact that some of the ostraca fit together (and so must have come from a single earthenware pot), it is thought that all the ostraca were written at Samaria itself by the scribes who were in the king's service. But which king? The ostraca do in some cases record that the delivery took place in the ninth or tenth year or in year 15 (one ostracon, no. 63, even possibly has the number 16 or 17) – but the king according to whose regnal years the dates are given is not indicated. At the time this was naturally self-evident but for us it is no longer so.

For the dating of inscriptions one can first of all examine the script. What is the shape of the letters and how does this relate to other inscriptions from this region? Specialists in this area date the script of these ostraca from Samaria to the first half of the 8th century B.C.E. (i.e. 800–750). One may also, for dating, take note of the context in which they were found: from what period does the stratum or layer in which these ostraca were found date? Although the excavation technique at Samaria in 1910 was, for the time, reasonably modern, it is not possible to get much precision on this point beyond the fact that the ostraca must be later than the reign of King Ahab (871–852) and earlier than the destruction of Samaria in 722/1 B.C.E.

There is, however, a further argument: not all the kings of the northern kingdom of Israel ruled for 15 years. Only a few candidates are available for the period within which the ostraca (on the grounds of script and archaeological context) can be dated: Jehoahaz (818–802 B.C.E.: cf. 2 Kings 13:1), Joash (802–787 B.C.E.: cf. 2 Kings 13:10) and Jeroboam II (787–747 B.C.E.: cf. 2 Kings 14:23). It must therefore have been one of these three kings – but who can guarantee that all the ostraca derive from the reign of the same king? In addition there is the fact that the group dated in the ninth or tenth year (both written out in full) differs somewhat as regards script and content from the group which derives from year 15 (in numerals). The possibility must therefore be kept open that the former group were inscribed, for example, during the reign of Joash, while the second group derives from the time of Jeroboam II. If that is the case, the texts can be dated precisely: the first ones in 794 and 793, the others in 773. 'Precisely' of course, in quotation marks, since (as already noted) there is still much disagreement about the chronology of the Israelite kings.

The significance of the ostraca

The importance of the Samaria ostraca lies above all in the topographical domain. On the basis of the names mentioned in the ostraca a good picture can be formed of Samaria's surroundings and of the extent of the districts which lay around the capital. The location of places which are mentioned in the Bible can be more precisely established with the help of these ostraca. Alongside the topographical information, the personal names are also of importance. In part these names also appear in the Old Testament, others are found, for example, on seals (see chapter 10), and some are unique. What is particularly interesting is that, alongside names of Egyptian origin, names referring to Baal occur as well as names including a shortened form of the name of the God of Israel, YHWH. The ratio is 8:11. Is there evidence of a mixed population here, Canaanites who worshipped Baal and Israelites who worshipped YHWH? But from the Old Testament itself it is clear that Israelites themselves gave their children names which included the element Baal, such as Jerubbaal (Judges 6:32), Gideon's other name, and the names of two descendants of Saul, Ishbaal (Ishbosheth) and Meribbaal (Mephibosheth) – and that even though Saul's other son was called Jonathan, which means 'YHWH has given'. Apparently no clear antithesis was yet felt to exist between the worship of Baal and that of YHWH, or one could also refer to YHWH himself by the title Baal (master).

Wine and oil destined for the courtiers of Jeroboam II – this recalls a passage in Amos, who must have been a contemporary of Jeroboam II (Amos 1:1). In the sixth chapter we read, among other things:

> Woe to those who are at ease in Zion,
> and to those who feel secure on the mountain of Samaria . . .
> who drink wine in bowls, and anoint themselves in the finest oils . . .
>
> (Amos 6:1a, 6a [RSV])

Anointing-oil and wine were a part of the luxury in which the court at Samaria lived, in contrast to the poverty of the less fortunate among the Israelites, a contrast that aroused the fury of the prophet. For the uncaring rich of Samaria, for whom servants worked the land, maintained vineyards and olive orchards and gathered in the harvest, Amos foretold a terrifying punishment. And in 722/1 B.C.E. the mighty stronghold of Samaria did in fact fall into the hands of the Assyrians, and (the upper class of) the population was deported from their homeland into captivity.

Chapter 5

THERE IS NO SILVER OR GOLD HERE: INSCRIPTIONS FROM JERUSALEM

One would have expected Jerusalem to have provided a wealth of archaeological discoveries, given the great importance of this city. Yet little of biblical Jerusalem has been brought to light. That is a result of the fact that Jerusalem has constantly remained an inhabited site. In particular very many ancient remains were destroyed by building activities in the Roman period, while today at many points excavations cannot be carried out without the demolition of existing buildings. Moreover in some places it is impossible for religious reasons to carry out archaeological research. This last factor has already caused some incidents.

The number of texts discovered is also limited. The most famous one, however, is especially interesting and takes us to the time of the Judaean king Hezekiah (715–697). In 722/1 Hezekiah, as crown prince, had lived through the death-throes of the Northern Kingdom of Israel at the hands of the Assyrians, after the last king, Hoshea, had risen in revolt against them. The capital Samaria was devastated and a part of the population was taken away into exile, the famous 'ten lost tribes'. This tragic episode is described not only in 2 Kings 17:4–7, but also, among other events, in various texts of the Assyrian king Sargon II, in which the following can be read:

> With the might of the great god, my lord, I fought against the inhabitants of Samaria, who had conspired with a king hostile to me to give no allegiance and to pay no tribute, and who delivered battle. 27,280 men, together with their chariots and the gods in whom they trusted, I captured . . . the city of Samaria I repaired, I made it greater than before. I made people from countries which I

had conquered live in it. One of my eunuchs I appointed as governor over them and I counted them among the inhabitants of Assyria.

Text on an ivory plaque

A portion of the booty which was taken away from Samaria to Assyria has been discovered in the Assyrian Fort Shalmaneser (Nimrud), including a Hebrew inscription on a fragment of an ivory plaque. The carving of ivory was a highly developed art in Israel: not for nothing is there mention in 1 Kings 22:39 of an ivory house which Ahab had built. The fragment found in Assyria displays such craftsmanship: the upper surface is highly polished and the letters are carefully inscribed. On the basis of the script this inscription is dated to the second half of the 8th century B.C.E., that is, shortly before the destruction of Samaria. So far as it is preserved the inscription can be translated as follows:

> May [YHWH] smash . . . after me: from great king t[o common man, anyone who] . . . comes and erases [this inscription].

The surviving part of this inscription thus comprises, according to a common practice, a curse-formula by which the attempt was made to compel respect in the following generation for the monuments and inscriptions of their predecessors.

The rebellion of Hezekiah

In spite of the terrifying warning which the annihilation of Samaria in 722/1 presented, Hezekiah too decided to risk a rebellion against Assyria. In this he did not act without forethought. He chose his time carefully, during a period when there were difficulties in Assyria itself. Moreover he took measures to strengthen Jerusalem in case of a siege by the enemy. The clearest account of these is found in 2 Chronicles 32:1–6, where it is reported that Hezekiah had all the springs and a stream blocked, so that the Assyrians would have no water. Further, 'he strengthened the walls of the city and constructed a new wall. In addition he organized the army and his supply of weapons.

Many see a connection between these measures and the construction of a water-tunnel, which even today still leads from the Gihon spring to the pool of Shiloah (=Siloam). The Gihon spring lies in the Kidron Valley east of the City of David, the oldest part of the city of Jerusalem, while the pool of Shiloah is situated to the south-west of the city of David (see fig. 10). That this tunnel was constructed on the orders of Hezekiah is reported in 2 Kings 20:20, 2 Chronicles 32:30 and Sirach 48:17, but in none of these passages is a connection made with Hezekiah's rebellion against Assyria. In itself that is a logical connection to make and possibly one can refer to Isaiah 22:9–11 in order to support this identification. During a siege the water-supply was a great anxiety for the besieged – a shortage of water would inevitably lead to surrender, and the rainfall in this region is too irregular to keep the cisterns (water reservoirs) always full. Therefore it was necessary to have permanent access to a spring with running water, even during a siege. Indeed, this spring needed to be secure enough to prevent an enemy having any opportunity to make it unusable by throwing a dead body in it or blocking it up with stones.

The problem of water supply was solved in various ways in ancient Israel: by means of shafts, tunnels and secret passages the attempt was made to guarantee permanent access to a spring, which normally speaking always lay outside the city. So Hezekiah's tunnel too could have served to bring the water of the Gihon spring to a safer place inside the walls.

However, the pool of Shiloah, where the tunnel comes out, is not within the walls of the city of David but just outside. That is very remarkable, for in this way the problem had only been moved. As a result it has reasonably been supposed that the western wall of the city, part of which has been discovered to the north and which must have been constructed in the time of Hezekiah, enclosed the pool of Shiloah too, before joining, at the southern end of the City of David, the older wall which surrounded this oldest part of Jerusalem. Proof for this assumption is lacking, however.

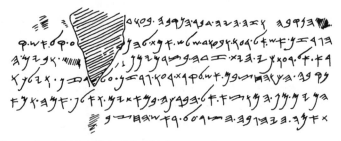

Fig. 9   Inscription from Hezekiah's tunnel

Another solution which is proposed takes its departure from a non-military function for Hezekiah's tunnel, which would explain why the outlet of the tunnel was not located inside the walls of the City of David. The tunnel is then connected with the water-supply for the new quarter to the west of the City of David. For those who had to draw water this tunnel probably signified a great improvement, seeing that they had to walk a much shorter distance than before. This hypothesis at the same time explains why in the biblical account no direct connection is made between the construction of the Shiloah tunnel and Hezekiah's measures to withstand the Assyrian siege.

Yet it seems rather improbable that Hezekiah would not have protected the outlet of the tunnel in some way or another against an enemy attack. Possibly the water did not end up in an open pool, as is the case today, but in a subterranean cistern. If that was the case this cistern must later, for example in the Roman period, have been exposed, so that the present arrangement arose.

The construction of the tunnel

The reason why Hezekiah had this tunnel constructed is not the only problem which this undertaking places before us. The ground-plan (fig. 10) makes it clearly apparent that the tunnel was not cut in a straight line but with something like an S-bend. As the crow flies it involves a distance of some 320 m., but because of the many bends in its line the tunnel measures approximately 534 m. Why so much extra work carried out?

This is an interesting problem and various explanations have been brought forward. Those who constructed the tunnel, it is suggested, did not want to dig beneath the royal tombs of Jerusalem and therefore made a detour; or they hit a hard layer of stone and had to change direction; or they followed a subterranean watercourse. None of these three theories corresponds to the actual situation. The possible royal tombs must have been situated high above the tunnel, the rock is not noticeably harder or softer in the places in question, nor have any traces been found of an older subterranean watercourse. The well-known archaeologist Kathleen Kenyon supposed that those who constructed the tunnel dug 'like moles'. But, seeing that the work was done with two gangs of workmen, one starting from the north and one from the south, and that at the point where they met the direction of digging hardly had to be adjusted at all, we must suppose that the digging was certainly not haphazard.

The most likely theory seems to me to be that the original intention was to work in a straight line but on second thoughts this idea was given up and a different plan was followed. If one consults the map (fig. 10) it can be seen that at

67

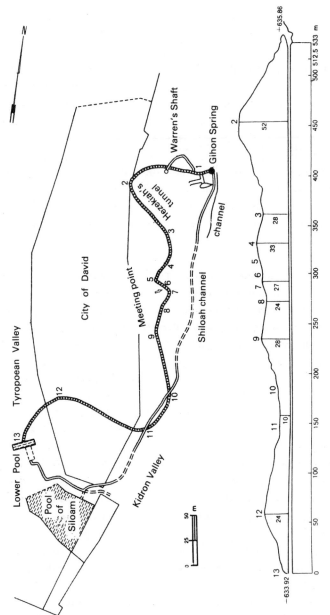

Fig. 10 Course of the Shiloah tunnel with transverse section (after *Jerusalem Revealed*, p. 76)

points 2 and 12 both gangs of workmen drastically changed their course. These points lie right on the boundary of the City of David, which lies on an elevated ridge. The southern group endeavoured to come out as quickly as possible from under the City of David in the direction of the Kidron valley. The northern group made a turn as soon as they came near to the city. A reason for this could have been that tapping from above was used as a way of signalling to determine the line, and that this kind of signal was no longer audible under the City of David, but was in the lower-lying area east of the city. In this way they would certainly have been forced to make a detour.

The theory of tapped signals from the ground above explains at the same time how it was possible for the work to be done accurately without a compass. The closing stages were naturally particularly tense. For there was the danger that the workers would cheerfully dig their way past each other, so that two tunnels parallel to each other would be produced. That of course had to be prevented and we can see on the map that between points 5 and 7 the line was continually adjusted so that the two tunnels actually met. In the end the two gangs were reassured by the sound of each others' pick-axes and could even shout out to each other. At the eventual meeting point it turned out that they hardly deviated from each other at all – a gigantic feat with the limited means available at the time.

The Shiloah inscription

The tension of that moment was recorded on an inscription, which was discovered by chance in the tunnel in 1880 by a schoolboy who went there to bathe. The inscription was located six metres before the outlet. After the lime deposit had been stripped off, casts could be made. That turned out to have been a wise precaution when, in 1890, the inscription was cut off the rock by a Greek who hoped to make a good sum of money from it. During this operation the inscription broke into separate pieces, which were confiscated by the Turkish authorities of the time. So the Shiloah inscription was finally brought to Constantinople, where the text was able to be restored with the help of the casts.

The inscription (fig. 9) can be translated as follows:

> [See] the boring. And this was the manner of the boring. While [the stonemasons were] still [striking with] the pick-axe, each man towards his comrade, and when there were still three ells (*1 .35 m.*) to bore thro[ugh, there was hear]d the voice of a man shouting to his comrade, as there was a *resonance* in the rock, in the south and i[n the nor]th. And on the day of the boring the stonemasons had struck, each towards his own comrade, pick-axe against [pick]axe. Then the water ran from the spring to the pool for 1200 ells (*540 m.*). And 100 ells was the height of the rock over the heads of the stonemasons.

This last statement is only partly true: the figure of 100 ells given here represents the maximum height reached at a few places. It is noteworthy that the rock-face on which the inscription was incised was levelled off over a larger area than was needed for the inscription itself, which only occupies its lowest part. Had it been intended to incise another inscription above it, or perhaps a drawing of the boring? But why then was this not carried out?

The text of the inscription itself also raises questions, however captivating the description of the scene is. When we dealt with the Mesha stele, it emerged that in a building inscription the king normally stands at the centre and that it is common for some of his other exploits to be recorded in the text. But here there is not a word about Hezekiah or any other official. The only people mentioned are the stonemasons, but it would have been most exceptional for them to have authorised the execution of the inscription.

The style in which the text is written is, moreover, rather like a narrative and that too is not typical of a building inscription. Hence it has with good reason been supposed that the text was transcribed from a Judaean chronicle. A pointer in this direction may be the fact that, as appears from 2 Kings 20:20, a passage about this tunnel stood in the Book of the Chronicles of the King of Judah. Unfortunately this source has not been preserved, so that we can no longer check the theory.

To return to Hezekiah once more: when he broke his treaty of vassaldom, the Assyrians did indeed come to subjugate Judah. In the face of greatly superior forces Hezekiah in the end chose the most sensible course: he paid a large tribute, in return for which Sennacherib broke off the siege of Jerusalem. A later legend told of an angel which was supposed to have killed 185,000 men of the Assyrians in one night (2 Kings 19:35), but probably it was gold and silver that saved Jerusalem.

Despite the fact that the land around Jerusalem had been devastated, the city of Lachish had been captured by Sennacherib (see p. 119) and many people had been killed or deported, there was great relief in Jerusalem, so great as to arouse the wrath of Isaiah. In Isaiah 22:1–14 we find the indignant words which Isaiah probably spoke on this occasion. After their frightening experiences the population turned to feasting, without having learned anything from what had happened to the land. The prophet therefore announces a merciless punishment, which did not, it is true, come to fruition in his own time, but did so in full measure a hundred years later (see further chapters 8 and 9).

The tomb of the royal steward

The continuation of Isaiah 22 (verses 15–19) has in fact been associated with a second inscription from the time of Hezekiah which has been found in Jerusalem. This relates particularly to verse 16, where Isaiah rebukes the royal steward Shebna in the following manner:

> What have you here and whom do you have here, that you have hewn out a tomb for yourself here, a hewer of his tomb on the height, a hacker of a dwelling for himself in the rock?

In this prophecy Isaiah rejects the custom which had probably come in under Phoenician influence, namely the provision already during one's lifetime of a monumental rock-tomb where one could be laid to rest after one passed away. Not to be buried was in antiquity a frightening prospect, because it was thought that the dead could find no rest outside a tomb. For this reason it was a bounden duty for the relatives to provide the deceased with a burial. In Sophocles' tragedy *Antigone* the heroine risks her life to throw a handful of earth on the corpse of her brother, which she was not permitted to bury. When a prophet in the Old Testament threatened someone with a frightening death, it was an end without burial. A death like that of Jezebel (1 Kings 21:23) or Jehoiakim (Jeremiah 22:19) was held in prospect. This is why people wanted to make sure in advance that the construction of their tomb was effected by themselves, insofar of course as they had the means for it. And it was precisely this latter point that aroused Isaiah's wrath.

In the village of Silwan (=Siloam or Shiloah) opposite Jerusalem the remains of such tombs can still be seen, which have been dated to the period 900–650 B.C.E. The workmanship of the tombs is so careful that it is presumed that the nobles of Jerusalem had reserved this region for their tombs. So even after death they remained together. Three types of tombs are distinguished: the most monumental type is interesting for this book, because inscriptions were also engraved on the façade of three tombs, inscriptions which are now, however, badly damaged. That is because the tombs were too attractive to allow the dead their peace. The tombs were reused in later times for different purposes, for which the entrances were widened. Even today they serve as storerooms or cisterns. No remains of the original contents of the tombs have been discovered. To that extent the prophecy of Isaiah has come to fulfilment.

As stated, little of the inscriptions can be read any more. On the so-called Monolith tomb the following decipherment has been possible (in translation):

> [This is] the tomb of Z . . . Whoever op[ens . . .]

Obviously we are dealing here with a curse-formula.

On the tomb of the royal steward two inscriptions were placed, which were discovered, cut out and sent to the British Museum in 1870 by the Clermont-Ganneau who was already mentioned in chapter 3. Only in the fifties of this century did the Israeli epigrapher N. Avigad succeed in deciphering the writing on them. The first is of little interest. According to Avigad it is to be translated:

> (Tomb)-chamber in the slope of rock.

But another translation is also possible:

> Tomb-chamber beside the tomb-[chamber] which was hewn out of rock . . .

According to this interpretation the inscription is incompletely preserved and it must be completed with 'which contains the body of X'. It will then be a case of a tomb with two chambers. This inscription related to the side-chamber, and the one which follows to the main chamber, where two bodies were laid to rest.

This second inscription is more extensive and alludes to the great anxiety of every owner of a tomb in antiquity, namely that a vandal in search of treasure might break open the tomb and violate the body. To avoid this, in Phoenicia for example, an inscription with an extensive curse-formula was placed on the tomb or the coffin – we saw an example of this in the first chapter (the inscription of Ahiram of Byblos). But the thought of treasure which a tomb might contain will often have been stronger than fear of death. That is why the second inscription from the tomb of the royal steward removes any illusion about the contents of this tomb in advance:

> This is [the tomb of . . .]yahu, who (was) over the (royal) household. There is [he]re no silver or gold, [on]ly [his bones] and the bon[es] of his slave-girl with him. Cursed be the person who opens it!

We are dealing here with the tomb of a very high official of the Jerusalem court: 'the one over the household' (*'ašer 'al habayit*) or 'the royal steward'. The title occurs a number of times in the Old Testament (cf. Genesis 44:1, 1 Kings 4:6, 16:9, 18:3; 2 Kings 10:5, 15:5, 18:18, 19:2; Isaiah 22:15, 36:3), and also on some seal-impressions, which remain to be dealt with in chapter 10. This responsibility comprised the supervision of the court and the king's possessions, but 'the one over the household' was at the same time a kind of Prime Minister. His role can be compared with that which the 'major domo' played in the Frankish Empire.

Because of a hole in the inscription we can only read the second half of the name of the owner of the tomb: -yahu. Now that is a very common ending for a Judaean name, and so we can make little headway with it. Two proposals for completing the name have been made: Hilkiyahu (Hilkiah) or Shebenyahu (Shebaniah). According to 2 Kings 18:18 and Isaiah 36:3 Eliakim the son of Hilkiah was royal steward around 700 B.C.E.: is it possible that he was the successor of his father? The name Hilkiah also occurs as that of the father of a minister of Hezekiah, of whom a seal-impression has been discovered (see chapter 10). This shows that Hilkiah may have been a leading figure of his time, if his sons fulfilled such important offices. But that this was his tomb remains no more than a guess.

The same is true for the completion of the name as Shebaniah, although I find it the more attractive. Shebaniah is the same as Shebna and that is precisely the royal steward against whom Isaiah directed the prophecy with which we began this section: the royal steward who had a tomb here for himself on the height. It would of course be a great coincidence if we have discovered the tomb of precisely this Shebna, but as far as the time is concerned it is a possibility: the inscription is dated to the time of Hezekiah, when Shebna was royal steward.

It may seem surprising that X-yahu was not buried with his wife but with his slave-girl. But the reader will be well able to imagine for himself the dramatic story which might lie behind this fact.

The Ophel ostracon

Less of a spur to fantasy is the ostracon which was found in 1924 on the Ophel, part of the south-eastern hill of Jerusalem, and can be dated from the style of the script to the end of the 7th century B.C.E. The text is incomplete and difficult to read. It concerns a list of names, accompanied by an indication of family and domicile, which points to a census aimed, for example, at the levying of taxes. Possibly the text may be translated as follows:

> Hezekiah, the son of Qore, in the field of the wool-combers; Jeho- . . .; Ahijah, the son of the wool-comber, in the valley of the 'hands' (= monuments); Zephaniah, the son of Qari, in the valley of the 'hands' . . .

The Ophel inscription

It is a particular pity that the fragment of a monumental inscription from the 7th century B.C.E., which was also found on the Ophel, can no longer be translated. There are twenty-five letters surviving on it, but nothing more can be made of it. The same is true for a fragment of a Hebrew inscription of the 8th or 7th century which was discovered in 1978 in the City of David. If these are the remnants of Judaean royal inscriptions (which is very possible), it is still unusually frustrating that so little has been preserved of them. It would of course be particularly important if a text from a Judaean king of the extent of the Mesha stele were ever to be found. I would however be very content with less, though I will draw the reader's attention to the view of E. J. Smit, who has written an article on ancient Hebrew inscriptions which ends as follows:

> The number of ancient Hebrew inscriptions is still quite small . . .
> The question . . . comes whether this fact is not precisely the result of a divine intention, namely that the history of the chosen people is in the Bible and that one should therefore not seek for or make reference to epigraphic evidence relating to it.

For the sake of epigraphic research we may only hope that E. J. Smit is not right.

Other ostraca from Jerusalem

On the Ophel yet more ostraca were found during the excavations of Kathleen Kenyon in the period 1961–1967. The first of this group derives from about 600 and was clearly a letter. Unfortunately only a part of it is preserved:

> . . . [fie]ld . . . And behold . . . for the people . . . field and . . .

Three other ostraca are concerned with deliveries of goods. One of them is especially worthy of note (at least if this is the correct interpretation):

200. *18 are counted to pay the tithe*

This is a case of a note that from 200 units 18 units were separated as a tithe. From this it appears that at this time tithes were paid in Judah, but that in so doing one was not very exact (9% instead of 10%). Possibly there is a connection with a measure which is ascribed to Hezekiah in 2 Chronicles 31:4–12, whereby the tithes for the priests and Levites were regulated. As far as the dating of this ostracon is concerned, this is possible.

In the western part of the city, which – as already noted – was probably enclosed by a wall in the time of Hezekiah, some discoveries of inscriptions have also been made, during the Israeli excavations which have been taking place since 1968 in the former Jordanian sector of Jerusalem.

The most important of these finds is a text written on a sherd (a piece of the shoulder of a storage jar) from the beginning of the 6th century B.C.E. – that is from immediately before the destruction of Jerusalem. There are three lines of writing on it but because the ink is very faded, it is now only possible to read the name Micaiah and *qoneres*. In the light of a Phoenician inscription of the 8th century from Karatepe we must divide *qoneres* into *qone eres*, 'creator of the earth', an epithet for God, which in a slightly modified form also occurs in Genesis 14:19. There the text speaks of El Elyon, God Most High, the creator (*qone*) of heaven and earth, in a conversation between Abram and Melchizedek, which takes place in Salem. Salem is probably another designation for Jerusalem.

The mention of Micaiah in the previous line indicates that we are not here concerned with a different god *qoneres* but with an epithet of YHWH, which was probably held in particular honour in Jerusalem. The question remains as to what the significance of this reference to God in the text is. Are we dealing here with a delivery of goods to the temple?

Tomb-inscription of Uzziah

Although it does not derive from the Old Testament period, it seems appropriate to conclude this chapter with the following inscription. (Two inscriptions from Jerusalem are dealt with in chapter 11.) This is a limestone plaque (35 x 34 cm.) which was noticed in the collection of the Russian monastery on the Mount of Olives and published in 1931 . The text, which is written in a slightly Hebraising form of Aramaic, is dated to the 1st century C.E.:

> To this place were brought the bones of Uzziah, the king of Judah
> – do not open!

This must refer to a secondary burial of the bones of the Judaean king Uzziah or Azariah (787–736). Posterity, however, took no notice of the emphatic warning at the end of the inscription. The stone was taken away and of the bones of Uzziah there remains no trace.

Chapter 6

THIS IS THE DOCUMENT ABOUT BALAAM, THE SON OF BEOR: NEW TEXTS FROM TRANSJORDAN

In an excavation things can go quite differently from what was expected when the work began. So when an expedition from Leiden University set off for Deir 'Alla in the Jordan valley in 1960, under the leadership of Professor H. J. Franken, to excavate part of the ancient mound (*tell*) there, no one had any idea that a textual discovery of the first rank would later be made here. They had come to gather a sufficient quantity of pottery from different periods to make a statistical investigation into the changes in the manufacture of pottery in this region through the centuries.

The story began with the discovery, during the excavation of quite a deep level, of the ruins of a sanctuary. On the basis of the finds it was possible to conclude that this sanctuary must be dated about 1200 B.C.E. That is precisely the period of the transition from the Bronze Age to the Iron Age in this region, the point in time when the people of Israel are mentioned for the first time in an Egyptian source. For that reason this period has a special place in the interest of Old Testament scholars: can archaeological discoveries give us a clearer picture of the circumstances under which the people of Israel came into existence? The discovery of a sanctuary from this period can therefore be of great importance for biblical research.

A part of the sanctuary was able to be uncovered: it lay in the area which had been chosen for complete excavation in the quest for pottery. The remainder, however, lay under deposits metres thick from later periods, which would have to be excavated systematically first, with each deposit layer differentiated stratigraphically, before the depth was reached at which the sanctuary lay. In an excavation the earlier layers of necessity lie lower down than the later ones.

Although in the meantime success had been obtained in the original aim of gathering sufficient classified pottery, this did not mean that work on the excavation was now finished. The important sanctuary could not be left any longer as it was. A larger part of the *tell* would have to be removed.

The discovery of the text

The excavators had to begin again at the top and work down again to greater depth. Before the layer of the sanctuary of 1200 B.C.E. was reached, however, they encountered another interesting structure, a complex network of different rooms. There a textual discovery was made which casts surprising light on the person of Balaam, namely 'The document about Balaam, the son of Beor.' The discovery was made in 1967, and since then scholars have been busy trying to understand what kind of building it really was that had been discovered. Is it also a sanctuary, not from the 12th but from the 8th century B.C.E.? In the past it was quite normal for temples to be built in the same place throughout the centuries. The finds to date (1989) have still not brought any clarity about this question, but the area in which the excavation of the *tell* is being carried on has had to be further enlarged. So archaeological research will continue for the time being at Deir ʿAlla for some years to come.

The discovery of *The document about Balaam the son of Beor* was itself a lucky chance. For this text is written on lime-plaster, a very brittle material which easily disintegrates into small fragments. Pieces of lime-plaster are quite often found during excavations and normally no particular attention is wasted on them. It was the same when the debris which originated in the rooms already mentioned, partly burnt and partly not burnt, was cleared. It was recorded that within this debris pieces of lime-plaster a couple of millimetres thick were found, but these were not kept any longer. Until, that is, the Arab foreman Ali, who had his training with the famous British archaeologist Kathleen Kenyon, discovered at a given moment that there was ink writing on the small pieces of plaster. The excavation was brought to a halt. It was the end of the season – a point in time when archaeologists are always working at top speed to finish everything in time, and any special discovery is greeted with little enthusiasm, and also precisely the point in time when particularly important discoveries are always made. Although therefore no one was standing around waiting to jump to extra work, it was realised at once that they could be dealing with a discovery for which the greatest ingenuity was going to be required to get it out of the ground in such a way that there would still be something to decipher. For the plaster could easily disintegrate still further and moreover the ink could come loose, with the result that the text would be completely lost.

With superhuman patience the fragments were conserved on the spot, while the spoil heap was checked for possible further written fragments. A gigantic job that was later continued in the museum. But all the work on the jig-saw puzzle produced a massive result, since it was possible to assemble the 119 fragments into a series of twelve interlocking pieces of plaster (combinations), which were legible, even if the meaning at times escapes us.

We are dealing with fragments: the whole text is no longer to be seen. We do not even know how extensive the text was, though it has been possible to make an approximate estimate of the length of the lines. In addition part of the text is no longer legible, because on the day that this building was destroyed it was raining! The plaster text, which must have been protected till then against the effects of the weather, was now exposed to the elements and the ink was washed away. Still what survived has turned out to be interesting enough.

A text on lime-plaster is quite an unusual discovery, though comparable texts have been found at Kuntillet 'Ajrud (see chapter 11). Probably, however, there were many more texts of this kind, but they have not been discovered because the writing-material is so delicate. A pointer in this direction is provided by Deuteronomy 27:1–4, 8, where the people of Israel receive the instruction to write all the words of the law on great stones, after these have been covered with lime.

The text from Deir 'Alla probably stood on a projecting part of a wall. It could be approached through a passage which was covered over by reed matting. A rather surprising place to put up a text. The text was partially framed by a red line, and the first words of each section were written in red ink instead of black, a custom that was already known from Egypt. There were also drawings beside it, among other things of a sphinx. As a whole it looks more like a copy from a text on papyrus than an inscription. The script used resembles most closely the Aramaic alphabet, even if there are some agreements with the Ammonite script, which (as we shall see below) is a development from the Aramaic alphabet; the language too exhibits the greatest agreement with Aramaic.

That is surprising, since Deir 'Alla lies in what was formerly Gilead, a region that was reckoned to be part of Israel. Was Hebrew, then, not spoken there? In addition there is no mention of the God of Israel anywhere in the text, only of non-Israelite gods. Furthermore, there is no indication that the writer of this text was an Israelite.

Now this is less remarkable than it looks. Gilead had a lively history. After it was colonised by Israelites, it was threatened from different sides. Aramaeans, Ammonites and

Moabites wanted to capture this fertile stretch of land. To begin with the Israelites were strong enough to resist these neighbouring peoples, but after the death of Ahab this changed (see also chapter 3). Specifically the Aramaeans were able to gain control of significant parts of the area. It is thus less remarkable that this text, which today is dated c. 760 B.C.E., appears to belong more to the Aramaean culture than the Hebrew. The region had probably already by this time completely lost its Israelite character, despite the fact that the Israelite king Jeroboam (787–747) seems to have succeeded then in reconquering Gilead. Finally this region was annexed by Assyria in 733, when a part of the population was deported.

What then is found in the text from Deir ʿAlla? Unfortunately the text is quite badly damaged and the interpretation of what has survived is much disputed. The first part (the 'first combination') remains the clearest and I will give a translation of it here, but with some reservations even as regards this section:

Combination 1
> [This is the doc]ument [about Bala]am, [the son of Be]or
> the man (who) is a seer of the gods.
> He! And the gods came to him by night
> [and they said to hi]m
> according to El's command
> and they said to [Balaa]m, the son of Beor, thus:
> He shall make . . . ,
> And Balaam rose up on the next morning . . .
> And he co[uld] not [eat.]
> [And he fa]st[ed,]
> and his people came to him.
> And th[ey said] to Balaam, the son of Beor:
> Why are you fasting?
> [And w]hy are you weeping?
> And he said to them:
> Sit down!

I proclaim to you what Shag[ar will do.]
And come,
see the work of the go[d]s!
[The god]s gathered together
and the Shaddai-gods took up their position in the assembly
and they said to Shagar:
You may break the bolts of heaven,
among your people (let) there (be) darkness and no brightness,
obscurity and not your . . .
You may give fear [by means of a] dark [clou]d,
but do not be angry for ever!
Truly the house-martin taunts the eagle,
and the you[ng] vulture the ostrich.
The st[ork] . . .s the falcon,
and the owl the brood of the heron.
The swallow . . .s the dove,
and the sparrow the . . .
And . . . stick.
In the place where the staff brought the sheep,
hares (now) eat the [g]rass.
. . .
. . , drink wine . . .
And the hyenas listen to admonition.
. . .
[A pupil] laughs at the wise,
and a poor woman prepares (herself) ointment of myrrh.
and a priestess . . .
. . .
. . .
Take heed, take heed, and take heed . . .
. . .
And the deaf hear from afar . . .
And everyone – they see the *oppression* of Shagar and Ashtar
. . .
. . . the panther.
The piglet hunts the . . .
. . .
. . . destructions and heaps of ruins.

'The document about Balaam, the son of Beor' – it would

have been a suitable title for the passage in Numbers 22–24, where (as is well known) the story is told of how Balaam was hired by the Moabite king Balak to curse the people of Israel – without success however, because Balaam was not in a position to curse this people: he could only bless them.

But what follows this title is not a text from the Old Testament; it is a story with much direct speech in it, in which a goddess plays the chief role. As for literary genre, this story is strongly reminiscent of the texts about prophets in the Old Testament in which narrative sections appear combined with prophetic speeches. Until recently it was thought that this type of literature only existed in Israel, but to judge from this text it is clear that Israel's neighbours also knew this literary genre.

A non-Israelite story about Balaam from c. 760 B.C.E. naturally casts an entirely new light on the passage in Numbers 22–24. Apparently Balaam was a well-known figure in Transjordan, who did not inspire only the biblical writers to record stories and prophecies. But was he actually a historical person and if so when did he live?

If the story in Numbers 22–24 had not been known, Balaam would have been dated on the basis of the Deir 'Alla text to the 8th century. The writer would have known him personally and wanted to record his deeds and especially his words for posterity, just as also happened with the great writing prophets of the Old Testament. As it is, the tendency is to assume that the text is speaking about a seer who lived 500 years earlier: at the time when the people of Israel were approaching the Promised Land.

This does not seem very probable to me. The Deir 'Alla text does not in the least give the impression of originating in or alluding to the distant past. In addition the Numbers narratives give an impression of non-historicity: in my view they date from the 6th century B.C.E. and are a reaction to the circumstances of that time. In the construction of the narratives the author used the person of Balaam, who had been known in Transjordan since the 8th century as a seer and a pronouncer of curses. In the untranslated part of the Deir 'Alla text Balaam is seen in his role as a great pronouncer of curses and the sparks fly around him. This very seer, who was held in such respect by the hated neighbouring peoples, is in the biblical story not in a position to curse Israel. He can only bless the people of God. Thus seen Numbers 22–24 belongs to the series of texts in the Old Testament which originated as a reaction to the hostile attitudes of Israel's neighbours to the east and south.

Elucidation of the text

To say that the first combination is a crystal-clear text would be somewhat exaggerated. But even so it is quite possible to follow the story. One night Balaam receives a visit from the gods, who have been sent by El, the Canaanite high god, who is identified in the Old Testament with YHWH. The message which they deliver to him is short and can no longer be reconstructed; but in the sequel Balaam has quite a lot to recount when he is asked about it. We also encounter this literary device, in which the divine message proves to be much more extensive the second time than originally appeared, in the Bible, e.g. in the book of Jeremiah.

As he fasts and weeps, Balaam receives another visit, this time from some men of his people. He tells them what is at hand. There has been an assembly of the gods, a well-known mythological motif, which also appears in Psalm 82:1. It is notable that the gods are specified as Shaddais, since Shaddai, in the combination El Shaddai ('God Almighty'), is equated with YHWH in the Old Testament. Clearly El Shaddai was in origin a designation of a group. Over against the Shaddai gods stands the goddess Shagar, who is greatly angered and harbours very sombre intentions. The gods permit her an outburst of rage, by which she may cause foul weather, but they urge her not to continue in her anger for ever.

It will be a hard time, Balaam declares, and he uses a series of pictures to describe the changes which are in store for the people, just as the Old Testament prophets too describe the coming doom in harsh colours. Not all the pictures are clear, but where flocks of sheep once grazed only hares will then be found.

It is the picture of the 'world in reverse', which is well-known from Egyptian literature, that he portrays. A time of catastrophe is distinguished – according to ancient oriental conceptions – by an interchange of roles in society: the poor take the place of the rich, the rich become beggars. In this case a poor woman prepares expensive ointment for herself, instead of this cosmetic being reserved for the rich. The wise are laughed at by their pupils (at least if that is the correct restoration; till now scholars have restored 'fools', but fools always laugh at the wise – so that cannot be an indicator of the 'world in reverse'). In the animal world too the roles are interchanged: the weaker animals taunt the stronger ones. The author disports himself here in a long enumeration of birds.

Balaam admonishes his audience: But take heed, for what is coming is terrible. Even the deaf shall hear the voice of the coming doom from afar. Just as with the Old Testament prophets, the announcement of doom is not a prediction of the future, but a summons to repentance. The people must take heed and put things in order again, then Shagar may desist from her anger.

Who is the goddess Shagar (the vowels are not certain), who can become so angry? Clearly in this region she was an important goddess, to judge from the role which she plays in this text. However, she is not known from other texts. But there is a reference in Deuteronomy 7:13, 28:4, 18, 51 to 'the *shagar* of your cattle and the *ashtarot* of your flocks.' In this text newborn animals are meant. Clearly the biblical writer uses the names of two goddesses in a secular meaning and Shagar was a fertility goddess just like the much better known Ashtart. It is also surprising that at the end of the first combination Shagar is mentioned with Ashtar, the male counterpart of Ashtart. Possibly Shagar had particularly the responsibility for looking after the fertility and the well-being of the (young) animals. Then it is understandable that she plays such an important role in the Deir 'Alla text, since the keeping of sheep was characteristic of this region. It is for that reason too that it is an utter catastrophe when – as Balaam declares – only hares can any longer be found in the land.

Although research on the Deir 'Alla text is still very much still on the move, the great importance of this text for Old Testament research is now well established. It is also evident from this text that the literature of the Old Testament is much less isolated within the literature of Palestine than was widely thought before.

Ammonite texts

To the east of Deir 'Alla lies the Jordanian plateau where the present capital city of Amman is situated. The name still recalls the ancient population, the sons of Ammon or the Ammonites. The remains of their ancient capital Rabbat Ammon also lie on one of the hills on which Amman is built: the Citadel.

Since 1961 texts deriving from the Ammonites have also been discovered there. They are written in Ammonite, a language that is related to Hebrew and Aramaic. In the 9th century an Aramaic script was used here, but about 750 B.C.E. they developed an Ammonite alphabet of their own. This did not last long, as in the Persian period there was a return to an Aramaic script. Compared with the Mesha stele and the Deir 'Alla text the inscriptions, ostraca and seals from the Ammonite region are much less interesting. Moreover the interpretation of the texts is sometimes still in dispute. It seemed unnecessary to include all Ammonite texts in this book, but the three Ammonite inscriptions which have been discovered do nevertheless add some information to our knowledge of the cultural background of the Old Testament and they will therefore be treated here.

The Amman Citadel Inscription

During excavations on the Citadel of Amman, where Rabbat Ammon once lay, an inscription was discovered in 1961. This stone was used in antiquity as building-material and because of this the text is seriously damaged. On the basis of the shape of the letters the inscription is dated around 850 B.C.E. – the text is thus approximately contemporary with the Mesha stele.

> [Mi]lkom [said to me]: Build entrances around . . . like everyone who besieges you, they shall die, surely die . . .
> . . . I shall lay waste, surely lay waste. And everyone who makes an entry . . .
> . . . And in every *pillared way* the righteous shall lodge . . .
> . . . (*untranslatable*) . . .
> . . . You shall fear the sons of the gods . . .
> . . . (*untranslatable*) . . .
> . . . peace for you and pe[ace *for your home*].

If the restoration at the beginning is correct, we are dealing here with a special kind of building-inscription, in which it is the deity who gives the king the command to have the building (a sanctuary?) erected in accordance with his instructions. In this way a divine authorization is claimed for

89

the building project. This kind of text is also known from Mesopotamia.

Milkom, the national god of the Ammonites, who also appears as such in the Old Testament, combines with his commission the promise that he will destroy the enemies who might besiege Rabbat Ammon in the future, and that he will bring peace to the king, if there is fear of the gods on his part.

This last requirement is already reminiscent of the Old Testament, though there the reference is naturally not to 'the sons of the gods' but only to one God. The text is however especially interesting, if we compare this inscription with Exodus 25–31, where God gives precise instructions about how the wilderness sanctuary is to look. This section of the Bible is undeniably much more detailed than the inscription, but the principle is exactly the same. The sanctuary is not designed by the builder, but by the deity.

The Tell Siran inscription

On Tell Siran, just outside Amman, a bronze bottle 10 cm in length was found in 1972. On the outside an inscription is written, which is still quite legible and is dated about 600 B.C.E.

> The works of Amminadab, the king of the sons of Ammon, the son of Hissil-el, the king of the sons of Ammon, the son of Amminadab, the king of the sons of Ammon, (are) the vineyard and the gardens and the *pools* and reservoirs.
> May he rejoice and be glad during many days and till distant years!

The text is clear, if it is assumed that by 'the works of Amminadab' are meant the vineyard, gardens, pools(?) and reservoirs which are mentioned in the sequel. We are then dealing here with a building-inscription which does not end (as is usual) with a curse-formula, but in a wish for blessing on the king.

It then remains a real puzzle why this text was not hewn on a stone, but is engraved on a bronze bottle. The bottle was carefully closed, so that its contents could still be examined. Apart from a no longer identifiable copper object they comprised different kinds of grass and seeds. This should make one think of a grave-offering, in which the grain could be a symbol for the food which the king is given in death. The wish for blessing at the conclusion of the text would in this case, however, be less suitable, so that the function of this bottle remains obscure.

Of the kings mentioned 'grandfather' Amminadab was already known from an Assyrian source. The detailed enumeration of his ancestors serves to underline the legitimacy of Amminadab's kingship.

The Amman theatre inscription

In 1961, during excavations at the Roman theatre in Amman, a piece of stone was found with a fragment of an inscription on it which is dated about 575 B.C.E.

> . . . -baal. I will build . . .
> . . . the sons of *Ammo[n]* . . .

However little of the text has survived, it is clear enough that we are dealing here with a fragment of an Ammonite building-inscription.

The Ammonite inscriptions thus fit closely into what was usual in the ancient Near East. They are building-inscriptions, in which the king stands in the central place. Only two fragments of this kind of inscription have been found in Israel (see pp. 57 and 76) and even in these cases we are not completely certain whether we are really dealing with royal inscriptions.

The most striking of these Ammonite texts is the Citadel inscription, because of the parallel with Exodus 25–31. From all these finds it becomes constantly clearer how Israelite culture formed a whole with the culture of the neighbouring peoples. That makes it all the more remarkable that in the course of the 8th, 7th and 6th centuries B.C.E. a theological literature came into existence in Israel which seems to break so completely with the general religious sentiment of the time. Israel was thus not a 'white crow' from the outset, as some people indeed believe, but in fact became one under the influence of the great prophets like Isaiah and Jeremiah.

Chapter 7

LET MY LORD THE GOVERNOR HEAR:
A PLEA FROM YAVNEH-YAM

In the study of antiquity it is always the people of the upper classes about whom we are informed. It was they, for the most part, who had the ability to write, or rather the scribes were in their service and wrote from the viewpoint of the prejudices of the ruling class. In the eyes of the rich the poor were for the most part not individuals but a group: the multitude, the masses. And they regarded the masses as stupid, unreliable, unstable and potentially dangerous. For the needs of this majority of the population there was only limited concern.

The texts too which we have encountered so far were produced for the benefit of the leaders of Israelite society: the king, the courtiers, the priests and the scribes. Even the so-called agricultural calendar from Gezer turned out to be written not by a farmer's son but by a future government official who will later have used the knowledge he acquired about the activities of a farmer to impose taxes on the king's subjects at the right time.

All the more remarkable, then, is the inscription which is the focus of this chapter: a plea of a farm labourer directed to the local governor. Thus in this text from the 7th century a member of the anonymous masses begins to speak. By itself this is a sign that at this time the use of writing must have greatly increased. No longer was it only the ruling classes who profited from this invention. Yet it is unlikely that this farm-labourer himself held the pen and wrote his petition on a large sherd (20 cm. by 7.5–16.5 cm.). The writing betrays a trained hand.

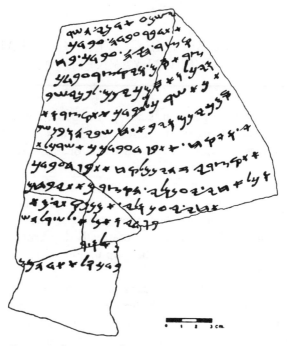

Fig. 11 Ostracon from Yavneh-Yam

We should therefore envisage the course of events as follows: the farm-labourer approached a professional scribe who practised his profession at the entrance to the local governor's residence. A similar scene can still be seen today at the ministries and other government buildings in Amman (Jordan): scribes sit on a stool behind a folding table with a writing-pad on it and nowadays quite often a typewriter as well. Around them wait a nervous group of people waving forms which have still to be filled in. To such a scribe the farm-labourer (we do not know his name, let alone the name of the governor to whom the petition is directed) will have explained what his business was. It was the job of the scribe to make out of this a convincing plea.

94

A confiscated cloak

The matter at issue was of great importance for the farm-labourer. His garment had been taken from him and he wanted to get it back. He could not easily do without his cloak; it served not only as a piece of clothing but also as a blanket. For just this reason a law was included in the Torah, which can be found in Exodus 22:25–26 (EVV. 26–27) and Deuteronomy 24:12–13:

> If ever you take your neighbour's garment in pledge, you shall restore it to him before the sun goes down; for that is his only covering, it is his mantle for his body; in what else shall he sleep? And if he cries to me, I will hear, for I am compassionate. (Exodus 22:26–27 [RSV])

God thus interposes himself in this text as guarantor for the poorest among the people: their outer garment must be given back by the creditor in the evening, then he may take possession of it as a pledge again the next day.

It thus appears that, as in this case too the garment had been confiscated by way of a pledge, the farm labourer had justice on his side and should have got his garment back before nightfall. That has not happened, as will be evident further on in the text. But he does not refer to this law in his petition, either because the law was for one reason or another unknown to him or because he found a submissive tone more suited to his wretched situation. Furthermore, he wanted to have his garment back not just for the night but for good. For he was innocent.

The petition is – as already stated – written on a large potsherd, which must have already been used before as an ostracon. Unfortunately in the course of time this sherd was broken and not all the fragments could be found at the time of the excavations, which took place in 1960 at a place 1.6km. south of Yavneh-Yam which has been given the name Meṣad

Hashavyahu. The text is thus no longer complete, and in addition some letters are unclear. As usual there is no unanimity about the interpretation of a number of difficult passages. However with some caution the text can be translated as follows:

> Let my lord, the governor, hear the word of his servant!
> Your servant is a reaper.
> Your servant was in Hazar Asam
> and your servant reaped
> and he finished
> and he has stored (the grain) during these days
> before stopping.
> When your [ser]vant had finished the harvest,
> and had stored (the grain) during these days,
> Hoshaiah came, the son of Shobai,
> and he took the garment of your servant,
> when I had finished my harvest.
> It (is already now some) days (since) he took the garment of your
>   servant.
> And all my companions can bear witness for me
> – they who reaped with me in the heat of the [harvest] –
> yes, my companions can bear witness for me.
> Amen! I am innocent of any gu[ilt].
> [Do give back] my garment,
> *so that I may be vindicated!*
> It is incumbent upon the governor to give ba[ck the garment] of
>   [his] serva[nt!]
> [And sh]ow pi[ty] on him!
> [And you should he]ar the [word] of your [ser]vant
> and you should not *be silent* [. . .]!

The text begins at once with an appeal to the governor to give a hearing to the farm labourer. The regular greetings-formula which one meets in letters from this time (see chapters 8 and 9) is lacking, as is an indication of the addressee. Clearly we are dealing here not with a letter, but with a written petition which was delivered directly to the governor. For this first line there is an excellent parallel in the

Old Testament. In 1 Samuel 26:19 David says to Saul:

> Now therefore let my lord the king hear the words of his servant.

The circumstances in which David found himself according to the story and the situation of the farm labourer are in fact comparable. David was being unjustly pursued by Saul; the farm labourer has unjustly had his garment taken away. Both ask for a hearing for their 'words', where it must be noted that the Hebrew word *dabar* can mean not only 'word' but 'matter', in particular 'lawsuit'. The king as well as the governor is requested to pay attention to the arguments which 'his servant' will bring forward to plead his case.

It has already been noted that we do not know the name of the governor. Even the precise nature of his responsibility is not fully clear. The Hebrew word *śar*, which is here translated 'governor', means in the first instance a military commander. In Exodus 18:13–26, however, it stands for a kind of judge. As far as this ostracon is concerned, it looks as if it here refers to the commandant of a fort, who also had the task of ruling the area around this fort and administering justice. The otherwise unknown place Hazar Asam (literally: 'village of the granary'), where the incident occurred, must have been in this area.

Dating

The fort which is involved here and in the ruins of which this ostracon was found (together with other, very fragmentary inscribed sherds) did not exist for long. It was built in the short period of expansion which Judah experienced under king Josiah (639–609 B.C.E.). In the period before that Judah was a vassal-state of the Assyrian empire. But during the reign of Josiah the power of Assyria greatly declined because of the Medes and an uprising of the Babylonians. By this means Josiah got the chance to make himself independent of Assyria and moreover to annex to Judah parts of the former northern kingdom of Israel. These areas needed of course to be militarily defended, not so much against the Assyrians, who had enough to do with the threat from the Medes and the Babylonians, as against Egypt, which also wanted to profit from Assyria's weakness.

The fort of Meṣad Ḥashavyahu was thus probably built by Josiah to defend the newly conquered coastal plain.

A surprising discovery during the excavation was the large quantity of East Greek pottery that was found in the fort. From this the excavator, J. Naveh, concluded that a group of Greek mercenaries must have been stationed here. At the time Greeks and Carians were in the service of the Pharaoh, but from the Arad ostraca (see chapter 8) it is evident that the Judaean kings too had Greek mercenaries at their disposal. The reason was that the Greeks had better equipment and better military technique than their contemporaries and this made them superior in war. They were also compelled by overpopulation in their homeland to make a livelihood elsewhere.

The fort, as already said, only lasted a short while; it was probably abandoned as soon as 609 B.C.E., when an abrupt end came for Josiah's nationalistic dreams. In that year the Egyptian Pharaoh Neco II decided to come to the aid of his former arch-enemy Assyria, when the Medes and Babylonians had already captured most of the Assyrian cities. Neco apparently had more to gain from a weakened Assyria that would be dependent on Egyptian aid than from the total disappearance of the kingdom from the map. So he set out with his army on his way to the last remnants of the Assyrian kingdom in Syria to offer some resistance to the Babylonians there. He no doubt hoped that in the event of victory the Assyrian king would grant him the region of Syria-Palestine, which had been lost by Egypt 600 years earlier.

However, Neco had to march with his troops through the

territory of Judah and this was not to Josiah's liking. He realised that in the event of an Egyptian victory Judah's independence would again be lost. Moreover, if he could stop Neco, he would certainly win the favour of the Babylonian king. Perhaps he would then leave Judah undisturbed. In spite of a warning from Neco to leave him alone, Josiah tried his luck in the plain of Megiddo, where the advance of the Egyptian army could most easily be brought to a halt. The result was his death. At this time (609 B.C.E.) the fort of Meṣad Ḥashavyahu must also have been abandoned.

The evidence of the plaintiff

But let us return to the ostracon. Although the text seems quite clear, on closer inspection much remains in the realm of uncertainty. In what relation did our farm labourer stand to the harvest? Was he a farmer who was obliged to work for a set period on the king's fields, or was he a day-labourer who had not finished his work? And who is Hoshaiah the son of Shobai? Was he a royal official who had to superintend the harvest? Or was he a foreman just as in Ruth 2:5–6 a servant appears who was set over the reapers? In Assyria the rule was that a foreman was responsible for the work of his reapers in the sense that if they did not turn up he had to pay a fine. If Hoshaiah had made a similar agreement, it is easier to understand that he did not pass by any means to get the work done and took away our farm labourer's garment to put him under some pressure in this way.

If I understand the text well, our harvester had in his own view fully completed his share of the work when Hoshaiah took these measures against him.

For the rule was that every reaper must harvest a part of the field – that was agreed in advance. He refers to this part as 'my harvest'. Clearly Hoshaiah did not agree with him when he claimed to have finished his work, and took his garment to prevent him going off straightaway. The incident had occurred some days before, but clearly Hoshaiah had not changed his opinion. That is why the harvester now addresses himself to the 'governor', who was held to be capable of forcing Hoshaiah to give back his garment to him.

For he is innocent, and if the governor does not believe him then his companions in the work, his 'brothers', will be witnesses on his behalf. They will say 'Amen' to the governor's questions: Yes, it is so. Our brother had completed his share of the harvest when Hoshaiah confiscated his garment.

The end of the petition is difficult to translate. In any case the harvester again makes an urgent appeal to the governor, in which he is asked not only to do what is right but to have pity. Clearly the harvester is not entirely convinced that the governor will agree with him (the translation of the Hebrew here is actually very uncertain).

Whether his plea was successful and the governor did not remain 'silent', or he let the matter take its course, we do not know. Of Josiah it was said by Jeremiah (22:16) that he secured justice for the poor and needy, but whether his subordinates followed this policy is an open question. Despite this the ostracon gives us a surprisingly vivid picture of the life of a poor farm labourer in Judah around 620 B.C.E. and the text makes clear what was meant in practice by the championing of the rights of the poor, to which the prophets called their contemporaries.

Chapter 8

TO ELIASHIB, AND NOW . . .
OSTRACA FROM ARAD

Tel Arad lies about 30 km. east of Beersheba and south of Hebron on the southern border of the ancient kingdom of Judah. The identification of Tel Arad with the Arad which is mentioned four times in the Old Testament (Numbers 21:1, 33:40; Joshua 12:14; Judges 1:16) is considered certain, which is unusual in the historical geography of the land of Israel.

From 1962 to 1967 inclusive, excavations were carried out here by the Israelis, and with good results. Not only was a large city of the Early Bronze Age found, but also a large fort from the Iron Age. The fort lay on the edge of the Early Bronze Age city, which was destroyed as early as 2600 B.C.E and after that was never rebuilt. When around 1200 B.C.E. a small village again arose on the mound, this brought an end to the hiatus in the occupation of the site. This hiatus is the more surprising, because the passages in the Old Testament already mentioned all allude to a time when Arad was no longer or not yet in existence (depending on your point of view).

This is a well-known problem in the history of ancient Israel. Jericho and Ai too were not inhabited or scarcely so in the time of Joshua. Clearly this was not known by the biblical writers when they composed these stories.

The citadel of Arad was built in the time of Solomon (around 950 B.C.E.), but was probably soon destroyed by Shoshenq I (=Shishak) in the course of his invasion of the land of Israel in 922 B.C.E. Shortly after this Arad was rebuilt, but during the so-called Syro-Ephraimite war in 734 B.C.E. it was probably destroyed again. Its third destruction occurred in 701 B.C.E. during the punitive expedition of the Assyrians against

Hezekiah (see chapter 5). During the reign of the Judean king Josiah (see chapter 7) the fort was completely rebuilt, but it did not survive long, as it was probably razed to the ground by the Egyptians around 609 during the conflict between Pharaoh Neco and Josiah, which was discussed in chapter 7.

The destruction of Arad which followed this one is so closely entwined with the history of the last years of the kingdom of Judah, that it is necessary to examine the latter more closely. After the death of Josiah the Judaean nobility promoted his son Shallum as king, who took the throne-name of Jehoahaz. This involved the passing-over of his elder half-brother Jehoiakim. However when Neco returned from his expedition against the Babylonians, he deposed Jehoahaz and replaced him with Jehoiakim, who paid him heavy tribute, for which he plundered the temple and his subjects (cf. 2 Kings 23:31–35). Thus Judah became a vassal-state of Egypt.

This Egyptian expansion did not last long. In 605 B.C.E. the Egyptians were defeated at Carchemish by the Babylonians. Then it was also time for Jehoiakim to change course: he became a vassal of Babylon, though without conviction, and from then on he paid tribute to King Nebuchadnezzar. Around 601 B.C.E. the Babylonian king made an attempt to enter Egypt, but without success. This was the occasion for Jehoiakim once again to change sides.

That turned out to be politically an extremely unwise manoeuvre, for when Nebuchadnezzar had restored the strength of his troops he struck back. In December 598 the Babylonians arrived in Judah and laid siege to Jerusalem. Then Jehoiakim died, being thirty-six years old. Was he killed by the enemy or murdered, or did he succumb to an illness? The sources are unclear on this. His son Jehoiachin (Coniah) succeeded him and tried to save what could still be saved, as will appear in the following chapter. At this time (February 597?) Arad must again have been destroyed.

At Tel Arad more than a hundred Hebrew ostraca (and also about the same number in Aramaic as well) were found, dating from the time of the earlier Judaean kings to the Persian period. This number is particularly impressive, but most of the texts are very hard to read or not very interesting in their content. Still these ostraca are important from an epigraphic point of view. Because of the many precisely dated destructions of Arad they are also easy to date. So they can offer a foothold for the palaeographical dating of other texts.

In view of the purpose of this book only a very limited number of ostraca from Arad come into consideration for discussion, namely nos. 1–5, 7, 8, 16–18, 21, 24, 40, 88 and 111, which was discovered in 1976. Of these ostraca the first group (up to and including no. 18) belong together: they are to be dated around 600 B.C.E. From this period also come nos. 21, 24 and 111. Ostraca 40 and 88 are older: ostracon no. 40 possibly from the end of the 8th century, no. 88 from around 608 B.C.E. We shall therefore deal with these two ostraca first.

Ostracon 40

Ostracon 40 is damaged: approximately a third of it is lost and the letters are partly blurred. The original editor of this and the other texts from Arad, Aharoni, gives in his edition a quite complete text but since much of what he thought he could read was based on guesswork, I shall only give a translation of what is definitely legible.

> Your sons Gemar[yahu] and Nehemyahu sen[d greetings to] Malkiyahu . . . And now . . . to whom . . . the man . . . with you . . . And behold: you know the . . . Edom . . . the day and . . . and he, he asked for the letter . . . The king of Judah knows . . . we cannot send . . . [thi]s is the evil which Edo[m] . . .

For all its fragmentary condition, this letter from Gemariah and Nehemiah, who were clearly subordinates ('sons') of

Malcijah, probably the commander of Arad at the end of the 8th century B.C.E., offers some historical information. The two writers of the letter were clearly involved in difficulties through the evil that Edom had done. By that a military invasion is possibly meant.

The Edomites were a people related to the Israelites and were reckoned as the descendants of Esau, Jacob's less fortunate brother. For a long time, though with interruption, they were subject first to Israel and later to Judah, but at the time when this ostracon was written they were once again independent. Because they themselves had great problems with Arabian tribes pushing into their territory, they accordingly endeavoured to capture the Negev from Judah – a purpose in which they were successful after the annihilation of the kingdom of Judah in 586 B.C.E. By doing this they brought on their heads a great number of prophecies of doom, of which a residue can be found in the Old Testament. But even in the 8th century B.C.E. there were conflicts between Edom and Judah and that is the background against which we should need to place this letter.

Ostracon 88

Despite the fragmentary state of this ostracon, no. 88 is particularly interesting:

> I, I have become king in . . . Strengthen (your) arm and . . . The king of Egypt for . . .

Since the ostracon was found on the surface of the *tell*, it can only be dated on the basis of the forms of the letters (palaeographically). From this we arrive at the second half of the 7th century. According to Aharoni we should have here the official proclamation of Shallum/Jehoahaz, when he succeeded his father Josiah in 609. He would be calling for a general mobilisation against Egypt: 'strengthen your arm' means something like 'mobilize'.

But according to Yadin, the famous excavator of, among other places, Masada, we are dealing here with a copy of a letter to Josiah written by the last king of Assyria, in which the latter seeks his permission for Neco II to march through his territory (see chapter 7). That is not very likely: the Assyrian king would surely have written in Aramaic. Moreover, how would the commander of Arad have been able to get his hands on a copy of a letter from the king of Assyria? Yadin is certainly right, however, when he observes that a proclamation by a Judaean king can of course never have been sent out on a potsherd: for that papyrus was used.

A more probable interpretation seems to be that it is a case of a scribal exercise, for which the pupil copied out parts of an official text. Whether the king in question, of whom the text speaks, was Jehoahaz cannot then be said with any certainty: it depends on the dating of the ostracon.

The archive of Eliashib

As already noted, ostraca 1–18 from Arad belong together. They derive from an archive in which the commander of Arad kept his current correspondence and memoranda. His name was Eliashib and to judge from seals that have been discovered he must have already held this position in the time of Josiah. He kept his current documents in a room in the casemate wall of the fort – at least this is where these ostraca were found. On the basis of ostraca 1, 7 and 17 it has been possible to deduce that Eliashib only kept the ostraca which he got for a short time. This was probably so that he could transcribe the contents of the ostraca, once a month, into his official report, for which he will have used papyrus. The ostraca which were discovered were thus preserved by accident, because Eliashib did not have a chance to work any more at his books before the Babylonians captured Arad in 597 B.C.E. The ostraca can therefore be precisely dated: they must derive from the beginning of 597.

Rationing

Most of the texts refer to rations, and the French epigrapher Lemaire has accurately calculated how much they amounted to. Reckoning was in periods of four or six days. The ration for four days consisted of 300 loaves and 2 *bat* (baths) of wine; for six days of 3 *bat* of wine and 1 measure of flour. This looks very like a sum like those which we were once set in primary school: if this information is given, how much wine did they get per day and how many grams of bread?

First the matter of the bread. It can be seen that for four days they got 300 loaves, but for six 1 measure (about 450 litres) of flour. Four days was clearly the maximum for bread to remain edible; that is why they got flour for six days, to bake their own bread. 450 litres of flour for six days is 300 litres of flour for four. To make one loaf of bread, therefore, one litre of flour was required.

On the basis of Jeremiah 37:21 it may be supposed that the ration of bread per day for one person was set at one loaf. A little calculation then shows that the rations in question must have been intended for a group of 75 people. Now this group gets 2 *bat* of wine for four days, or half a *bat* per day. The size of a *bat* is disputed. According to some it is 24 litres, according to others 40–45 litres. On the basis of this ration-list the second looks more probable than the first. Otherwise the recipients of these rations would have had to be satisfied with a sixth of a litre per day, and for a Mediterranean people that is quite inconceivable.

It is interesting that this group of seventy-five persons are described as the Kittim, since this is the Hebrew name for parts of the Greek-speaking region. The name is probably derived from Kition in Cyprus. Originally, therefore, it was a designation for Cypriots. Eventually all Greeks were called Kittim, while in later Hebrew this became the name for the Romans (cf. Daniel 11:30). In this text Greeks must be meant, who, just like the inhabitants of the fort near Yavneh-Yam, (see chapter 7) were in the service of the Judaean king as mercenaries.

Ostracon no. 1

> To Eliashib. And now, give to the Kittim, of wine 3 *bat*, and write the name of the day. And what (is) still (left) from the first flour you shall have *loaded up*, 1 measure of flour to make bread for them. From the wine (intended for) the mixing-bowls you shall give.

This is the first of the series of ostraca with orders about the delivery of rations. In view of the authoritarian style they must originate from a superior of Eliashib whose name is not stated. 'Write the name of the day' is reminiscent of Ezekiel 24:2:

> Son of man, write the name of the day, yes of this day exactly!

Eliashib thus receives the order to note the date of the delivery in his official book-keeping. What exactly is meant by 'the first flour' is not entirely clear. Is it a reference to flour from the first grain harvest of the year, or flour from the first milling? It has already been noted that the Kittim baked their bread themselves, as the rations came for more than four days at a time.

By way of a P.S. the giver of the orders adds a note that the Kittim are to get special wine intended for mixing-bowls (*kraters*). That means that he had spoken first of wine in general. but evidently realized that this could give rise to misunderstanding. For the Greeks were accustomed to mix their wine with water, so the wine had to be stronger than the normal Judaean wine.

Ostracon no. 2

> To Eliashib. And now, give to the Kittim 2 *bat* of wine for the four days and 300 loaves. *And fill (with) sparkling wine*, and you shall hand (them) over tomorrow. Do not delay! And if there is still some wine vinegar, then you shall give (it) to them.

This time provisions for four days. The choice of wine again causes the giver of the order concern. This time it is not for krater-wine but for sparkling wine, that is to say, wine that is still fermenting. This type is mentioned in Deuteronomy 32:14 (cf. Psalm 75:9). At the end he speaks of wine vinegar, which could also serve as a drink (cf. Ruth 2:14; Psalm 69:22; Matthew 27:48 and parallels).

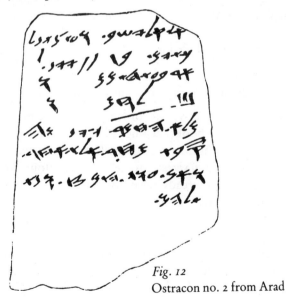

Fig. 12
Ostracon no. 2 from Arad

Ostracon no. 3

> To Eliashib. And now, give from the wine 3 *bat*. And Hananiah
> has ordered you (to go) to Beersheba with the load of a pair of asses
> and you shall oppress (them) *with oppression*. And count the
> wheat and the bread and you shall take. . .

This ostracon is possibly written by a different hand from the
two preceding ones. One who gives orders to Eliashib is mentioned by name. It has indeed been presumed that this Hananiah
wrote the previous two letters or had them written. As we shall
see later that is less likely on the basis of ostracon no. 16.

The note is not entirely clear. Eliashib is to deliver wine,
count wheat and bread, and take something else (oil?) to send.
There is in addition a reference to an order of Hananiah. Has
this already reached Eliashib before, or is the writer of the letter
passing it on now, so that the translation should be: 'orders you
now'? This is grammatically possible.

As regards the load of a pair of asses, 2 Samuel 16:1 gives a
fine parallel:

> And a pair of saddled asses, and on them two hundred loaves, and
> a hundred raisin-cakes, and a hundred summer fruits and a pitcher
> of wine.

The ration, which is intended for David in this passage of the
Bible, seems more attractive to me than the provisions with
which Eliashib's subordinates had to be satisfied.

As indicated the translation 'and you shall *oppress* (them)
with oppression' is uncertain. If it is correct, it must mean
something like 'spur them on well'. It then makes the same
point as 'Do not delay' in ostracon no. 2.

The back of the ostracon was inscribed with the rest of the
order, but unfortunately it is no longer legible.

It is surprising that Eliashib here appears as an ass-driver –
that does not fit with the assumption that he was the
commander of Arad at this time.

Ostracon no. 4

> To Eliashib, Give to the Kittim 1 (pitcher) of oil; seal (it), and
> 1 *bat* of wine – give it to them.

This ostracon is written by another hand again. Once more an
order to supply the Kittim with rations. The olive-oil is to be
sealed. That involved the placing of a lump of wet clay on top
of the pitcher filled with oil, on which impressions were made
with a seal-stone. When the clay had become hard, the pitcher
could not be opened without breaking the seal (on seals see
further in chapter 10).

Only when sending olive-oil is Eliashib instructed to seal
the pitcher. This indicates that olive-oil was an expensive
product, more so than wine.

Ostracon no. 5

> To Eliashib. And now, send away from yourself some of what
> (remains) from the f[i]r[st] flour, [t]hat . . . flou[r to make] bread
> for . . . who . . . to you the *ti[the]* . . ., before the new moon is
> past. And the rest . . . the work . . .

The text is too damaged to provide much information any
more. The mention of the tithe is very interesting (if the
restoration is correct; see above also, p. 77), and so is the
passing of the new moon. The latter recalls Amos 8:5:

> When the new moon is past,
> then we can deal in grain,
> and the sabbath,
> then we can open the grain-sales.

Clearly in this period the day of the new moon was similar to
the sabbath and no business could be transacted on such a
day. We shall return to this issue after introducing the next
ostracon (no. 7).

Ostracon no. 7

> To Eliashib. And now, give to the Kittim for the tenth (month) on
> the 1st of the month until the sixth of the month 3 *bat*. And you
> shall write this before your face on the second of the month, in the
> tenth (month). And se[al] oil . . .

The most interesting aspect of this ostracon is the instruction
to record this delivery for six days not on the day itself but on
the following day. Clearly no deliveries were supposed to be
made on the first day of the month (cf. ostracon no. 5 and
Amos 8:5), but attempts were made in this way to keep the
breach of religious rules off the record. Compromise over the
commandments is clearly a phenomenon of all periods.

Ostracon no. 8

> To Eliashib. And now, give to the Kitti[i]m 1 measure of gra(in)
> from the thirteenth of this month to the eighteenth of this month
> [and] wine, 3 *bat* . . .

The lower half of this ostracon is illegible. The quantities
mentioned agree with what preceded. Once again here a
period of six days.

Ostracon no. 16

> Your brother Hananiah sends greetings to Eliashib and greetings
> to your house. I bless you by YHWH. And now, after I departed
> from your house, I sent 8 shekels of [si]lver to the sons of Gealiah
> [by] the ha[nd of A]zariah, and . . . with you . . . the silver . . . and
> if . . . send Nahum and you shall not send . . .

In this ostracon, which is difficult to read, it is immediately
striking how the tone differs from the preceding ostraca. Not
an abrupt command, but an expansive formula of greeting.
Hananiah also refers to himself by name, as was usual in a

letter (and still is). Clearly the preceding ostraca were not letters but memoranda.

Although the possibility cannot be excluded that Hananiah was really a brother of Eliashib, it is more probable that we are here dealing with one who was his equal in rank. It is natural to identify this Hananiah with the Hananiah to whom reference was made in ostracon no. 3. If there were two Hananiahs among Eliashib's associates, they would surely have been distinguished by their patronyms. The Nahum who is mentioned could be the same as the Nahum who appears in ostracon no. 17 as Eliashib's subordinate. Although the details are no longer clear because of the poor condition of the ostracon, the subject here is a delivery of silver. Hananiah has made this after being with Eliashib; clearly Eliashib had asked him about it and now Hananiah renders his account of the matter. He also reports who brought the silver. Eliashib now knows whom he can hold responsible if the silver should not arrive.

Ostracon no. 17

> To Nahum. [And] now, come to the house of Eliashib, the son of Eshiah, and you shall take *from there* 1 (pitcher) of oil and send (it) *to them* quickly and seal it with your seal.
>
> *Verso* (different hand). On the 24th of the month Nahum gave oil into the hands of the Kitti: 1 (pitcher).

This ostracon breaks the regular sequence. Not Eliashib but Nahum is the one to whom the memorandum is addressed. There must have been a special reason why there is change from the usual overseer. Eliashib may have been ill or away (for example at Beersheba: see ostracon no. 3), so that Nahum had to take over his duties. From the fact that Eliashib is now officially designated with his patronym but Nahum not, we can deduce that Nahum was Eliashib's subordinate. He certainly has access to Eliashib's house and possessed a seal of his own.

On the back Nahum noted down that the instruction was carried out, so that Eliashib could record it in his account-book. So it was not necessary for him to state which month was involved. It is certainly striking that the givers of orders always seem to be in a hurry; in that respect there is nothing new under the sun.

Ostracon no. 18

> To my lord Eliashib. May YHWH ask after your welfare. And now, give to Shemariah a measure *of flour* and to the Kerosite you shall give a measure *of flour*. And as regards the matter about which you gave me orders, that is in order. In the house of YHWH (*verso*) he remains.

The writer of this ostracon treats Eliashib with more deference than usual; clearly it does not come from a superior. In view of the fact that the unknown writer gives Eliashib an order, but has also received one from him, they must have been equal in rank. The designation 'Kerosite' recalls Ezra 2:44 and Nehemiah 7:47, from which it appears that it refers to temple-servants. By 'the house of YHWH' either the temple in Jerusalem or the local sanctuary at Arad is meant. Who the person is who now remained in the house of the Lord after the execution of Eliashib's command we do not know. For the fact that someone is being accommodated in the temple Nehemiah 13:5 offers a parallel.

Ostracon no. 21

> Your son Jehokal sends greetings to Gedaliah [the son of] Elyair and greetings to his house. I bless you by YHWH. And now, see, my lord has done . . . May YHWH fulfil for my lord. . . Edom . . . everyone who . . . and if still . . .

This incomplete ostracon was discovered in a room in the vicinity of the find-place of the ostraca addressed to Eliashib and it must date to the same time. Just as in ostracon no. 40 we have here a letter from an inferior (the 'son') to a superior. The subject of the letter is unclear. The reference to Edom is interesting.

Ostracon no. 24

(*Recto illegible*)

(*Verso*) From Arad 5 and from Kin[ah] . . . and you shall send them to Ramat-Neg[eb by the ha]nd of Malcijah the son of Qerabur, and he is to transfer them over into the hands of Elisha the son of Jeremiah, in Ramat-Negeb, so that nothing happens to the city. And the word of the king is with you upon your soul. See, I have sent (this advice) to warn you today: the men (must be) with Elisha, so that Edom does not come there.

The first eleven lines of the ostracon are illegible, so that we do not know who the writer is and who is meant by 'you'. The ostracon was found on the western slope without any archaeological context. In view of the form of the letters it comes from the same time as the ostraca addressed to Eliashib. His name can perhaps still be read on the front side of the ostracon.

The ostracon was clearly sent by the supreme command of the army, since the order is presented as an instruction from the king which must be carried out on pain of death (that is the meaning of 'the word of the king is with you upon your soul'). A transfer of troops was decided upon in connection with a threat from the Edomite side, in which the important city of Ramat-Negeb was in danger. For this they were ready to remove troops from Arad and Kinah (unless we have here a special levy additional to the normal garrison units). This group of soldiers is to be taken under the leadership of Malcijah to Elisha, who was clearly the commandant of

Ramat-Negeb. This place is mentioned in Joshua 19:8 and 1 Samuel 30:27. The severe tone of the letter shows what a critical situation already obtained.

Ostracon no. 111

In the summer of 1976 three more new ostraca were discovered during restoration work at the fort of Tel Arad. Of the three sherds only ostracon no. 111 is a letter. Unfortunately this ostracon is in a very fragmentary condition, so that much remains obscure.

> And during the watch . . . he was very [af]raid and I shall giv[e] . . . [And if] he is taken, we shall send back word . . . The horse was . . . And to hear . . . water . . .

It looks as though we have a military situation here: possibly a deserter or a spy was being pursued. But perhaps I am getting too carried away by fantasy.

The last two ostraca differ noticeably in their atmosphere from the preceding ones. They show that the mood in Judah became more tense when the Babylonian threat became more concrete. In the next chapter we shall be looking at the final destruction of the kingdom of Judah by the Babylonians.

Chapter 9

WHO IS YOUR SERVANT – A DOG? OSTRACA FROM LACHISH

The first siege of Jerusalem by the Babylonians ended surprisingly, because on 16 March 597 Jehoiachin, together with his family and part of the Judaean aristocracy, gave themselves up to the enemy. In this way he prevented the total destruction of his land and moreover saved his own life. For the Babylonians abstained from further reprisals, when they had deported the king, his court and some other Judaeans (among whom was the prophet Ezekiel) to Mesopotamia and seized much booty.

In the so-called Babylonian Chronicle, an important survey of the history of Mesopotamia which is preserved in part on various clay tablets, this event is described as follows:

> The seventh year (of King Nebuchadnezzar), the month Kislev: The king of Akkad (=*Nebuchadnezzar*) mobilised his army and marched against Ḫattu (*Syria*). Over against the city of Judah he encamped. On the 2nd of Adar he captured the city and took the king prisoner. A king of his choice he appointed to rule over it. He took heavy tribute and brought it to Babylon.

Then Judah was allowed to remain in existence as a vassal-state under a new king whom Nebuchadnezzar had appointed. The Assyrians had also employed this practice when dealing with rebellious vassal-states: the reigning king was deposed and replaced by one who was more trustworthy. If he also rebelled, then the territory was annexed and placed under a governor. The choice of Nebuchadnezzar fell on an uncle of Jehoiachin, Mattaniah, who on his accession took the name Zedekiah. Probably Nebuchadnezzar hoped that Zedekiah, who was a full brother of Shallum/Jehoahaz who had at an earlier time been deposed by Pharaoh Neco II, would also follow an anti-Egyptian policy. And anti-Egyptian at that time meant pro-Babylonian, since there was no longer any middle way open.

Nebuchadnezzar's choice, however, was an unfortunate one. Zedekiah was too weak a personality to resist his pro-Egyptian advisers. In 589 B.C.E. Zedekiah halted the payment of tribute to Babylon and hoped to withstand the inevitable Babylonian punitive expedition with Egyptian support. A vain hope: in January 588 Nebuchadnezzar marched into Judah and laid siege to Jerusalem while his troops ravaged the country. An Egyptian attempt to relieve Jerusalem forced the Babylonians to break off the siege for a short time but – as the prophet Jeremiah had foretold – they came back. When the situation became entirely hopeless, Zedekiah made an attempt to escape. He was overtaken at Jericho and punished in a horrifying manner. His sons were put to death before his eyes and then he was blinded, so that the murder of his sons was the last thing he saw. Afterwards Zedekiah and a large group of exiles were deported to Mesopotamia, and Jerusalem, with its temple, was destroyed (586 B.C.E.).

From these last years of the kingdom of Judah comes a group of ostraca which give a picture of the tense situation. We refer to a discovery made at Tell ed-Duweir, approximately half-way between Ashkelon and Hebron. This *tell* is identified by most archaeologists with the city of Lachish, though not by all. The excavation of the *tell* began in 1932 under the direction of the British archaeologist J. L. Starkey. The operations came unexpectedly to a standstill when Starkey was killed by Arabs in 1938. It was nearly another thirty years before Israeli archaeologists could resume the work again, first under the direction of Y. Aharoni and then under D. Ussishkin.

Eighteen ostraca were found in 1935 and three in 1938. The

Fig. 13 Reconstruction by Gert le Grange of the Assyrian attack on Lachish by means of a siege-ramp (from *IEJ* 30[1980], 184).

Israeli excavations have also produced ostraca, but they are less interesting and will not be dealt with further here.

Tell ed-Duweir is an extensive mound of ruins and the excavations have shown that already in the Early Bronze Age a settlement began here. In the Middle and Late Bronze Ages a fortified city existed here, which was destroyed at least twice. Probably in the time of Rehoboam (926–910 B.C.E.) a fortress was erected on the site (cf. 2 Chronicles 11:9). The city was surrounded by a double wall, and there was a palace and a sanctuary ('high place').

We can form a clear picture of how Lachish must have looked, because the Assyrian king Sennacherib had his capture of the city in 701 B.C.E. (see chapter 5) portrayed in a room of his palace at Nineveh. The various reliefs give a vivid picture of how the Assyrians went to work when they besieged a fortified city. The fact that Sennacherib had the military undertaking represented on stone in such a detailed way proves that this siege made a great impression upon him.

Dating of the ostraca

But the ostraca which are dealt with in this chapter do not come from the time of Sennacherib: they were written shortly before the destruction of Lachish by Nebuchadnezzar. They were discovered in the vicinity of the main gate of the fortress; probably they lay in the sentries' guardroom at the moment of the destruction. Some of the ostraca give nothing more than a list of names, possibly of persons whose arrival in Lachish was noted by the sentries. They could also refer to rations. Most, however, are letters, even though a few are too fragmentary to be discussed here. Therefore only ostraca 2 to 6 and 9 will be translated and discussed.

Even more than with the ostraca considered earlier the lack of further data makes the interpretation of these texts particularly difficult. The name of the sender and the date are missing and the circumstances in which these memos were written is not clear to us. On the basis of ostracon no. 3, where a sender is in fact named, some investigators suppose that all the ostraca originate from a certain Hoshaiah. This however, does not seem very likely. The ostraca were not all written by the same hand, and the writer of ostraca nos. 2, 5 and 6 employs a deferential idiom which Hoshaiah in ostracon no. 3 never displays. Ostraca 2, 6, 7, 8 and 18 certainly do belong together, as they are sherds from a single object of pottery.

The name of the addressee we know well: he was called
Yaosh (or Yaush), but he is not known to us from other
evidence. In view of the deferential formulae which the
writers use with reference to Yaosh it can be presumed that he
occupied a high position: probably he was the commandant of
Lachish. Hoshaiah was then the commander of a military post
which was under the jurisdiction of Yaosh; this is true for the
writer of ostracon no. 4 too. In ostracon no. 9 there is in
addition a reference to a certain Shelemiah, who came as a
messenger.

We can fix the dating of these ostraca in 589 or the beginning
of 588. For it appears from the ostraca that the atmosphere is
very tense, but Judah is not yet under Babylonian control.
The city is still in contact with Jerusalem (ostraca nos. 4 and
6), while the Judaean army commander can still travel freely
to Egypt (ostracon no. 3). The sherds must therefore have
been inscribed in the period between Zedekiah's refusal to pay
tribute and the Babylonian invasion in January 588.

Ostracon no. 2

> To my lord Yaosh. May YHWH let my lord hear tidings of peace,
> right now, right now!
> Who is your servant – a dog, that my lord remembers his
> [se]rvant? May YHWH *make* my l[or]d *remember* a matter which
> you do not know (any more).

This letter is rich in deferential expressions, but it is not
immediately clear what its factual content is. What does the
writer mean by his pious wish that YHWH may refresh his
superior's memory? Or should we translate the end in a
different way? The proposals that have been made to date for
this are, however, not very convincing.

The description which the writer of the letter gives of
himself is not a very complimentary one. Dogs were and are

regarded as contemptible creatures in the Near East. We have here a deferential formula which also occurs in the Old Testament. In 2 Samuel 9:8 Mephibosheth makes it even stronger, when addressing David and saying:

> What is your servant that you address yourself to a dead dog such as I am?

A dead dog is of course even more contemptible than a living one.

In this and the other letters it is striking how often there is an appeal to YHWH. This shows – think also of the many theophorous names in these texts, mostly ending in -iah – that reverence for YHWH was very great in Judah at this time, despite the accusations of the prophets that the people did not go far enough in the service of YHWH.

Ostracon no. 3

> Your servant Hoshaiah sends (a message) to repo[rt to] my [lo]rd Y[a]o[sh]. May YHWH let my lord hear tidings of peace and *tidings of good fortune.*
>
> And now, please open *the eyes* of your servant about the letter which *my lord* sent to your servant yesterday evening. For the heart of your servant has been sick since your sending (of the letter) to your servant and because my lord says: 'You do not know how to read a letter!' As YHWH lives, if ever someone has tried to read a letter for me! And also every letter which comes to me – when I have read it I can repeat it [la]ter down to the last detail.
>
> And it has been reported to your servant, saying: The commander of the army Coniah, the son of Elnathan, has come down to go to Egypt. And (*reverse*) as regards Hodujah, the son of Ahijah, and his men, he has sent (a message) to take (them) from here.
>
> As to the letter of Tobiah, the servant of the king, which came to Shallum, the son of Yada, from the prophet, saying 'Take care!' – your ser[vant] has sent it to my lord.

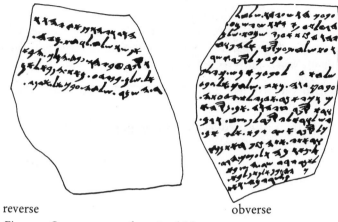

reverse   obverse

Fig. 14   Ostracon no. 3 from Lachish

This long letter contains some interesting information, though it is particularly regrettable in this very case that Hoshaiah was not rather more explicit in the information which he gave.

First a politely packaged sign of discontent. The letter which Yaosh had sent to Hoshaiah the previous evening had met with his displeasure. It was clearly stated there that Hoshaiah could not read; possibly Yaosh was dissatisfied with the execution of a command which he had earlier conveyed to Hoshaiah in writing. With little sense of humour Hoshaiah now protests in detail that he always reads his letters himself and like a pretentious schoolboy he adds to this that afterwards he can repeat them out of his head (if that is the correct interpretation of this difficult passage in the Hebrew).

Hoshaiah also attempts to arouse some feelings of guilt in his superior, by saying that he became ill after reading the letter and he requests that he should once more explain what he intended by his words. This last remark is diplomatically packaged by Hoshaiah: his lord is asked to open his eyes about the letter. He must have understood it in the wrong way; Yaosh certainly intended it quite differently.

Then Hoshaiah comes to the point. He has received a report that the commander of the army (probably the supreme commander is meant by this term: cf. 1 Samuel 17:55; 1 Chronicles 25:1) is on his way to Egypt and clearly he has passed a military post. From there he has sent a message to Hoshaiah to provide him with men under the leadership of a certain Hodujah (at least that seems the likeliest interpretation of the ambiguous Hebrew here). It may be supposed that the army commander was now coming through a region which was less safe and he needed an extra escort which Hoshaiah was to provide for him.

It is, however, surprising that no army commander called Coniah is mentioned in the book of Jeremiah, seeing that most of the leading Judaeans of the period are mentioned in this book of the Bible. Coniah is on the way to Egypt and that must of course be connected with the advance of the Babylonian troops. The supreme commander must have carried on consultations with the Egyptian army command about how to make a stand against the troops of Nebuchadnezzar. But beyond this it must have been Coniah's job to induce the Pharaoh to intervene militarily in favour of Judah.

Possibly Coniah had a letter with him from king Zedekiah to the Pharaoh. How such a letter might have looked we can imagine rather precisely since the discovery of a papyrus in 1942 at Saqqara (near Memphis). This is a letter from an otherwise unknown ruler Adon, who asks the Pharaoh for military support in connection with the advance of the Babylonian troops. The letter, which is dated around 600, is written in Aramaic, the diplomatic language of the time (see pp.13–15):

> To the lord of kings, the Pharaoh, your servant Adon, the king of
> . . . . . . of heaven and earth and Baalshamayn, [the] god . . .

[may they make the throne of] Pharaoh as permanent as the days of heaven. What . . .

[The troops] of the king of Babylon have come; they have *reached* Aphek, and . . . They have taken . . .

For the lord of kings, the Pharaoh, knows that [your] servant . . . to send an army to save me. Let him not leave me in the lurch . . . And your servant keeps his goodness (in his mind). And this region . . . a city governor in the land, and they have *exchanged* a *document* . . .

The first question which this text raises is, of course, who is this Adon? His kingdom must have lain in the vicinity of Aphek, otherwise he would not have felt himself to be so threatened by the Babylonians. Now chance has it that there are five places by the name of Aphek situated in this region, so that it remains a matter of guesswork, but perhaps Adon was the king of one of the Philistine city-states. The details of the text are no longer clear because of its many lacunae, but the overall sense is clear enough: the Pharaoh should now send an army to his faithful vassal, if his territory is not to be annexed by the Babylonians.

Whether it was the result of this mission of Coniah's or not, Egypt did in fact send an army (cf. Jeremiah 34:21; 37:5, 11), but as already noted, without success.

The third subject of Hoshaiah's letter concerns another letter, which he sends along with this ostracon. It is a letter of a certain Tobiah, which has come to Shallum. A warning was clearly involved here, as the letter begins with 'Take care!'. Tobiah is described as the servant of the king, which means that he occupied a high position at the court (see p.142).

But what is the role of the prophet and which prophet is meant? Some have certainly thought of Jeremiah (to be exact, Yirmeyahu), the more so as there is also mention of a prophet in ostracon no. 16, and his name ended in -yahu (the rest of the name is illegible). But this is no more than a guess: there were various prophets at that time. The Hebrew is, in addition, ambiguous here: it can imply that Tobiah wrote the letter, but also that it concerned him. This letter came, in one way or another, into the hands of an unnamed prophet. Subsequently, this prophet sent the letter to Shallum. We do not know how the letter came into the hands of Hoshaiah. Did Shallum give it to Hoshaiah, or was he arrested and the document found on him? Or had the letter already been in the possession of Yaosh, and been sent by him to Hoshaiah in the same way as he sent other letters? The latter is more probable but, as already stated, it is unfortunate that Hoshaiah expressed himself here so briefly; it would have been interesting if we had possessed more information about the role of the prophet, in connection with the question about how much the prophets actively interfered in Judaean politics.

Ostracon no. 4

> May YHWH let my lord hear right now tidings of good fortune! And now, in accordance with everything about which my lord sent (a message), so has your servant done. I have written in the *column of the papyrus* in accordance with everything about which [my lord] sent (a message) [t]o me. And as regards (the message which) my lord sent concerning the matter at Beth-harafid: there is no one there.
>
> And Semachiah – Shemaiah has taken him and made him go up to the city. And your servant – I can[not] send the *witn[ess* at once] from here, but only in the course of tomorrow morning.
>
> And let him know that we ourselves are watching the smoke-signals from Lachish according to all the signals which my lord gives, for we cannot see Azekah.

It is a great disadvantage in the interpretation of this letter too that we do not know the contents of the message to which the writer of the letter is responding. Probably this ostracon too was intended for Yaosh, although his name is not mentioned. The writer was one of his subordinates, who was stationed at a post outside Lachish, for at the end of the letter he talks about his careful watching of the smoke-signals which rise from Lachish. He was thus not in Lachish at that point in time.

The writer, after his good wishes, reports that he has carried out all that he was commanded to do and that he has written down what he had to record in his official journal. At least that is probably how the Hebrew should be translated here; the relevant word means literally 'door', but it occurs in Jeremiah 36:23 in the sense of 'column of a sheet of papyrus'. It is the irony of history that this official journal, for which the expensive material papyrus was used, has perished, but that the notes on sherds have in part survived the ravages of time.

The second command concerned an investigation of the otherwise unknown place Beth-harafid. Possibly the writer had to check whether this place Beth-harafid had already been evacuated in connection with the approach of the enemy. Or was Yaosh already expecting advance troops of the Babylonian army to be there?

The third command was carried out by Shemaiah, clearly a subordinate of the writer. He has arrested a certain Semachiah and brought him to Jerusalem, possibly for trial. But a witness was still lacking and this man can only come on the following day (at least if this is the right interpretation of the Hebrew). What Semachiah had done we do not know. The first word of the last part of the letter can be translated in different ways: 'He knows', 'he shall know', 'he knew' or 'let him know'. The last of these seems the most probable to me. He (= Yaosh?) should reckon with the fact that the writer can indeed see the smoke-signals from Lachish, but not those from Azekah. Formerly it was common to interpret this section as if it read: 'We can *no longer* see Azekah'. Azekah would thus have already fallen into the hands of the Babylonians. This remark was connected with Jeremiah 34:7, where it says that at a given moment only Jerusalem, Lachish and Azekah still remained in the hands of Zedekiah – the other fortified cities of Judah had already been captured by the Babylonians.

This interpretation, however, is untenable, as 'for we can *no longer* see Azekah' requires an additional word in the Hebrew, which is not present. Therefore this remark can only mean that Azekah was not visible from this military post, for example because it was too far away.

The context of the end of this letter is probably the following: Yaosh wrote to the commanders of the various military posts around Lachish and Azekah to ask whether they could see the smoke-signals which had been, as an exercise, sent up from Lachish and Azekah. In connection with the threatened Babylonian attack it was of great importance to know whether by means of smoke signals rapid communication according to a pre-determined code ('all the signals which my lord gives') could be achieved. Smoke-signals fulfilled in antiquity (together with fire-signals by night) the same function as the telegraph in our own time: thereby it could be signalled whether a particular individual or an army was approaching or that a decisive moment had arrived (cf. Judges 20:38, 40). The writer replies that all is well as far as Lachish is concerned but that the signals from Azekah are not visible to him.

In Jeremiah 6:1 there is also a reference to a smoke-signal. Jeremiah is speaking here about the disaster which will come from the north to punish the people who will not repent:

Blow the trumpet in Tekoa,
And raise a smoke-signal above Beth-haccerem!

His words came true and the smoke-signal which had been anxiously awaited must undoubtedly have been sent up when the Babylonian troops trod Judah under foot.

Ostracon no. 5

> May [YHWH] let my [lo]rd hear [tidings of peace] and good fortune [right now], [right] now!
>
> Who is your servant – a dog, that you have [s]ent *such* let[ters] to your servant? Your servant now sends the letters back to my lord.
>
> May YHWH let you see *the harvest in good fortune* this year! May Tobiah br[in]g royal seed to your servant!

In this ostracon the unknown writer is thankful for the confidence which his lord (Yaosh) has placed in him by sending letters to him, which he now returns.

At the end, after a pious good wish, he comes to the central point of his letter. It is harvest-time (around June 589 B.C.E.) and he enquires anxiously whether he will indeed receive the grain placed at his disposal by the king. Whether Tobiah is the same person as the servant of the king of that name, who is mentioned in ostracon no. 3, we do not know for sure, because Tobiah is referred to here without further specification. It seems less likely to me, because it would be less appropriate for a subordinate to refer to a high official by his name alone, without adding his title or the name of his father.

Ostracon no. 6

> To my lord Yaosh. May YHWH let my lord see this time (in) peace!
>
> Who is your servant – a dog, that my lord sent [the lette]r from the king [and] the letters from the princ[es, sayi]ng, 'Read this!'? And behold the words of the [*princes*] are not good, because they weaken [your] hand [and *let si]nk* the hands of the me[n] . . . He knows . . . My lord, should you not write t[o them saying: wh]y have you done thus, and especially in Jerusalem? Be[ho]ld against *the king* [and against his house] ha[ve you done this thing]. As YHWH your God lives! truly since your servant read [the] letter[s], there was *n[o rest* for your] se[rvant].

This ostracon is broken into three pieces and in addition the letters are badly faded, which makes the reading of them uncertain. I can therefore only give the translation printed above with some reservations. That is in this case particularly regrettable, because this letter gives interesting information about the political divisions in Judah on the eve of the Babylonian invasion, a topic which is known from the book of Jeremiah. From there it is clear that there were two groups: a pro-Egyptian party which had always aimed at a rebellion against Babylon and a pro-Babylonian party, which saw no future in such a rebellion but advocated submission to Babylon. Supporters of both parties could be found among the members of the royal household. Between the two parties stood King Zedekiah, without the ability to follow a way of his own. Although he eventually inclined towards the pro-Babylonian party, he could nevertheless not stand up to the pro-Egyptian princes, which led to the ruin of his land and his family, as we saw earlier.

From this ostracon too we hear of criticism of the policy of the governing circles in Jerusalem. Yaosh, who as commander of Lachish received letters from the king and the princes, had sent these on to his subordinate to learn the latter's opinion. Clearly he attached value to the judgment of his servant, although he was – according to his own words – of no more value than a dog. The subordinate is very impressed by the fact that his opinion is being sought and becomes unusually excited about what he has read. He no longer has a moment's rest.

In this agitated mood he advises Yaosh to write a letter to the princes, in which he would point out to them the consequences of their actions, which are having a harmful influence on the king and his house.

But what actions were involved and what was in the letters which the princes sent? The only thing which we learn about this from this document is that the words of the princes will weaken Yaosh's hands. The expression in the Hebrew also occurs in Jeremiah 38:4, where the princes (!) say to King Zedekiah that Jeremiah must be put to death, because he weakened the hands of the warriors and of the whole people with the words that he spoke.

This passage in Jeremiah, which alludes to the same time and situation as this ostracon, forms such a close parallel to this text, that some scholars have proposed to restore not 'the words of the [princes]', but the words of the [prophet]' with Jeremiah then being referred to as 'the prophet'. The context of the letter, however, makes this restoration improbable: there is nowhere any reference to a prophet, but there is to the letters of the princes. The translation which has also been proposed, 'to weaken the hands of the Chaldeans and bring to rest the hands of the enemies', is even less suitable in the context, seeing that criticism has been levelled in this very letter against the statement concerned and that would not have happened to words which would bring the Babylonians to their knees.

We must therefore conclude that the princes wrote letters, obviously independently of the king (which is in itself a sign of how weak Zedekiah's position was), letters with a clearly defeatist content. In view of the parallel with Jeremiah 38:4 we must be dealing here with princes who belonged to the pro-Babylonian party and saw no profit in a continuation of the struggle against Nebuchadnezzar. The subordinate of Yaosh is, however, in total disagreement with their present policy. They would have harmed the king's position and deserved a reprimand which Yaosh evidently could give – so powerful was his position.

Thus this letter gives a penetrating picture of the confused situation in Judah in the time of Zedekiah, despite the uncertainty which exists regarding its proper interpretation.

The wish which the writer expresses at the beginning was certainly not fulfilled. There were no tidings of peace and the anxiety which the writer had was not without justification.

Ostracon no. 9

> May YHWH let my [lor]d hear ti[dings] of peace and [good fortune]!
> And [now, give] bread 10 and [win]e 2.
> Send back [to] your servant a word by (*reverse*) the hand of Shelemiah, (to say) what we must do tomorrow.

After the interesting ostraca which we have dealt with before, this simple request for rations and orders for the following day comes as an anti-climax.

However difficult the interpretation of some passages in the Lachish ostraca is, these texts are so far the most interesting historical documents to have survived from ancient Israel itself. When they are placed alongside the biblical books of Jeremiah and 2 Kings, one gets an unusually fascinating picture of a tragic period in Israel's history, when they went to meet the coming disaster with their eyes open. Neither the warning of Tobiah from Lachish ostracon 3 to 'take care', nor the many prophecies of Jeremiah could prevent it.

Chapter 10

BELONGING TO BERECHIAH, THE SON OF NERIAH: SEALS, SEAL-IMPRESSIONS AND WEIGHTS

Far and away the largest group of inscriptions from ancient Israel is formed by seals, stamps, weights and inscriptions on pottery. These texts consist mostly of a single word or a couple of names; for that reason they are less interesting for the subject of this book. That is not, however, true for all these texts: hence the inclusion of this chapter containing a small selection from a multitude of finds.

In contrast to the ostraca (inscribed sherds) there are also texts which were written on pottery while it was still intact, sometimes before, sometimes after firing. Some examples of this have been and will be discussed in other chapters: by way of supplementation some more of this kind of inscription are treated here, which mostly give the place of origin or the owner of the relevant item of crockery.

Thus at Hazor remains were found of a jar from the 8th century, on which had been inscribed: 'Belonging to Makbiram' – clearly the name of the potter or the owner. It has, however, been proposed to read a 'd' in place of the 'r' – then a Hebrew word is obtained which can be translated as 'for the food-servers'. The jar would then have been intended for the service of food. Two more similar discoveries were made at Hazor.

At el-Jib (generally identified with Gibeon) a large group of jar-handles with inscriptions on them were found between 1956 and 1959. In nearly every case the place-name Gibeon comes first, followed by two or more personal names. These are probably from wine-jars of approximately 700 B.C.E. The inscriptions may relate to those for whom the wine was intended or to the producers. In the latter case they are comparable to the labels on present-day wine-bottles.

La-melek stamps

A special problem is formed by the storage-jar handles on which a LMLK-stamp has been impressed, of which more than a thousand examples have already been discovered. There has been much discussion and writing about the function of these stamps, without agreement being reached, though certainly a few things have become clearer than they were when the investigation began.

Thus we now know that these stamps were used in the kingdom of Judah in the monarchy period. From the Israeli excavations at Lachish (see chapter 9) it has even become very probable that these stamps were only in circulation in the second half of the 8th century. One thinks then especially of the reign of Hezekiah.

It has also become clear that these stamps were impressed before firing, in some cases also accompanied by a seal-impression of a private person. Moreover the number of seals used was very restricted: there are thought to have been eighteen to twenty-four stamps, with which all these impres-

Fig. 15   LMLK-stamp impression from Ramat Raḥel

133

sions would then have been made. No such stamp, however, has yet been found.

At the top always stands LMLK, which can probably be best translated as 'royal'. Beneath comes a symbol: a winged scarab (which can be portrayed in different ways) or a winged sun-disc. A scarab is a representation of a dung-beetle, which in Egypt was the symbol for the life-giving force of nature. Scarabs were used in Egypt as seal-stones or amulets, but they were popular throughout the region surrounding the Mediterranean Sea. In Palestine too many scarabs have been discovered. It is therefore not at all surprising that this symbol was chosen. The winged sun-disc was also a popular motif at this time and one to which no religious significance need be attached.

Under this comes a place-name, and in fact always one of the following four: Hebron, Socoh, Ziph and an as yet unidentified place-name which should possibly be pronounced Mamshit. It is a remarkable selection, since apart from Hebron it is definitely not the most important places in Judah which appear on these stamps. What can the reason have been why only these places are mentioned?

The search for an answer has been made with much inventiveness: we may be dealing with administrative centres, where taxes were collected; or they may have been the four royal store-cities, or the location at this particular time of the royal vineyards. But the wide scatter of the jars with these stamp-impressions makes these suggestions less probable. A more attractive proposal seems to be that we are dealing here with four pottery manufacturing centres, one at Hebron, one at Socoh, one at Ziph and one at Mamshit. However, study of the clay from which these jars were made has proved that they must have been manufactured at a single place. The four place-names on the handles must, therefore, have a different significance which for the present escapes us. The LMLK mark can indeed perhaps be explained as due to a wish to indicate in this way that the jar concerned remained royal property. If that is so, it also becomes clear why on certain jars three concentric circles were incised (thus after firing). That could be a sign that the jar had been released for private use. The seal-impressions of private persons which sometimes accompany the *la-melek* stamp-impressions could be those of officials who acted as inspectors.

Potters in the service of the king are mentioned in 1 Chronicles 4:23, but there the places named are Netaim and Gederah.

In any case the theory of royal potteries is certainly consistent with the fact that the handles belong to a single type of oval jar, some 65–70 cm high and with a maximum breadth of 45 cm. At the broadest point four handles were attached, which could carry stamp-impressions. The jars served for the transport of wine or olive-oil. Probably such a jar (containing approximately 45 litres) was hung on either side of an ass. Of course they could also be used as storage-jars.

Weights

On weights there is sometimes an indication of what weight is involved, just as is also the case now with old-fashioned pairs of scales. A hundred inscribed weights of this kind have been discovered, which will not be further treated here (see also p. 3). What is very surprising is that weights with the same inscription seldom weigh exactly the same in grams. Clearly not much precision was customary then in this matter and it has even been supposed that less scrupulous traders used different weights with the same inscription depending on the circumstances. A passage like Amos 8:4–6 gives this supposition more reality. Here the oppressors of the people determine, among other things, to do the following:

> to make the ephah small, and the shekel great, and to bend the
> scales deceptively.

The ephah and the shekel are units of measurement, the ephah
for measuring produce and the shekel for measuring payment.
Hence the point of making the ephah 'small' and the shekel
'great'.

Seals and seal-impressions

At present there are about 750 seals or seal-impressions which
have been published – a respectable figure, while every year
new ones are discovered. The large number is, however, not
so surprising when it is borne in mind that seal-stones are of
course quite durable and many people would have found seals
necessary for financial and legal transactions.

For the impression of a seal functioned like a signature, as
proof that a letter was genuine (cf. 1 Kings 21:8) or to
guarantee the validity of a contract of sale (Jeremiah 32:10).
We have already seen, on p. 110, that it was also possible to
seal a jar by impressing the seal-stone on a stopper made from
soft clay, so as to prevent misappropriation.

The seal-stone was worn on a cord around the neck or
wrist; a seal could also be fixed to a ring. As can be
understood, a seal was an important possession for its owner,
and he or she could give it as a pledge. When Judah in Genesis
38:18 cannot at once pay Tamar her fee he gives her his staff
and his seal as a pledge – with which she is eventually able to
save her life, as the reader who knows the Bible well will be
able to remember.

The seal of the king was naturally of great value. Whoever
had it in his hands was in a position to prepare decrees or
write letters on behalf of the king (compare again 1 Kings

21:8). When the Pharaoh appoints Joseph to be his right-hand man, he hands over his seal to him (Genesis 41:42).

The type of seal-stone which was in use in Israel and Judah resembles, as far as form is concerned, those which have been found in other parts of Syria-Palestine. But it is a distinctive feature of the Hebrew seal-stones that from the 7th century B.C.E. they only rarely display a pictorial design. The seals from the 8th century do indeed have, as well as a text, such a design with motifs that are well-known from Phoenician art. But on the later seals – but for some exceptions – there are exclusively letters. Could this have something to do with the ban on images?

The short inscriptions on the seals mainly contain the name of the owner, which may be accompanied by that of his father. So they give information about Hebrew proper names. A small group is interesting for the reason that they also give information about the profession of the owner of the seal. This is mostly a matter of high functionaries of the king and in this way we gain more insight into the various top jobs which were distributed by the king in the kingdoms of Judah and Israel. We shall give a brief summary of these seals. I have indicated the numbering for each seal proposed by G. I. Davies (see bibliography) – from nos. 1 to 438 this corresponds to the arrangement adopted by the Italian scholar F. Vattioni (see bibliography).

Royal steward (lit. 'who is over the house')

This important position at court has already been discussed on p. 74. Seal-impressions of various royal stewards have been discovered:

Belonging to Gedaliah [w]ho is over the house.

(seal-impression; Lachish; around 600 B.C.E.; Davies, no. 149)

The Gedaliah who is mentioned here is plausibly identified with the Gedaliah who was appointed as governor of Judah by Nebuchadnezzar after the fall of Jerusalem in 586, but was shortly afterwards murdered (cf. Jeremiah 40:1–41:15). However, in the Old Testament it is not said that before that Gedaliah had occupied the position of royal steward, so the identification remains uncertain.

Belonging to Adonijah who is over the house.

(three seal-impressions which derive from two seal-stones; provenance unknown; 7th century; Davies, nos. 501–502)

This royal steward Adonijah is not known to us from the Bible. We see that a high official had more than one seal-stone at his disposal.

Belonging to Nathan who is [o]ver (the) house.

(seal-impression; provenance unknown; 7th century; Davies, no. 503)

The royal steward Nathan is also not known to us from the Bible.

The chief of the corvée (lit. 'who is over the corvée')

It was probably David who, following what was customary among kings at that time, first imposed corvée service on the people of Israel. He had a special functionary for this: Adoram, 'who is over the corvée' (2 Samuel 20:24). In the time of Solomon this functionary was called Adoniram (1 Kings 4:6, 5:28 – RSV 5:14). Solomon's son Rehoboam also had such a functionary who was again called Adoram. The latter had a tragic finale to his life. When the Israelites had repudiated their allegiance to Rehoboam, the king had the senseless idea of sending this very Adoram to meet the rebels.

For it was precisely the corvée which formed one of their most strongly-felt grievances: it involved compulsory unpaid work for the benefit of the king, the coordination of which was the responsibility of Adoram. The inevitable happened: Adoram was stoned by the angry mob.

The Old Testament does not mention this position again after this, but we now know, through the discovery of a seal-stone, that at any rate in the late monarchy it was still in existence.

> Belonging to Pelaiah, (the son of) Mattitiah.
> (*reverse*) Belonging to Pelaiah, who is over the corvée.

(perforated seal-stone, quartz; provenance unknown; end of 7th century; Davies, no. 782)

The owner of this seal thus had the choice between two seal-impressions. If he impressed the reverse side, his position was also given. Did he use one side of the seal for his private correspondence and the other for official business? Or did he, after obtaining this position, have his title engraved on the reverse side of his seal-stone?

The governor of the city

This position is mentioned in the Old Testament in connection both with Samaria (1 Kings 22:26) and with Jerusalem (2 Kings 23:8). The task of this high official was the administration of the capital. No actual seal-stone has been discovered, but there are two impressions from the same seal with the text 'the governor of the city' (Davies, no. 402). In addition there is a design on it in Assyrian style, from which one can see how this official was received in audience by the king. The surprising thing is that the name of the official does not appear on this seal: did several people make use of it? Date: end of the 7th century B.C.E.

The title possibly also appears on storage jars from the 8th century, which were found at Kuntillet 'Ajrud (see p. 158).

The son of the king

The reader will be surprised to find that 'the son of the king' appears here as the designation of a profession. Probably we are in fact dealing here with the title of an official who, among other things, was in charge of justice (cf. 1 Kings 22:26; 2 Kings 15:5; Jeremiah 36:26 and 38:6). Possibly the person concerned was indeed a member of the royal family, so that the title could also be taken in a literal sense. At any rate Jotham, the son of the king (mentioned in 2 Kings 15:5), later became king over Judah.

> Belonging to Manasseh, the son of the king.

(seal; provenance unknown; 8th or 7th century B.C.E.; design: star and moon; Davies, no. 209)

There has been an understandable wish to identify this Manasseh with the later king Manasseh (696–642), especially because a star and a half-moon are portrayed on the seal and in 2 Kings 21:5 it is said of Manasseh that he built altars for the whole host of heaven (=astral deities) in the two forecourts of the temple.

The design on this seal-stone could thus symbolise both the moon-god Sin and the goddess Ishtar/Ashtart. It would then be necessary, of course, to suppose that Manasseh, who became king at the age of twelve, might already have had his own seal when he was still a boy – and that is not very likely.

> Belonging to Jehoahaz, the son of the king.

(seal; provenance unknown; end of 7th or beginning of 6th century; design: a cock in fighting pose; Davies, no. 252)

It has been assumed that we are here dealing with a seal of the later Judaean king Jehoahaz (see p. 102). The cock on this seal-stone resembles the cock which appears on the seal of Jaazaniah (see p. 142). Could this be a family coat-of-arms?

Belonging to Gaaliah, the son of the king.

(seal-impression; Beth-zur; end of 7th century or beginning of 6th century; Davies, no. 110)

This name does not occur in the Old Testament. A second seal-impression of this Gaaliah was discovered later. This impression (Davies, no. 506) comes, however, from a different seal-stone, so that it looks as if this official too had more than one seal-stone at his disposal.

Belonging to Elishama, the son of the king.

(seal; provenance unknown; 8th-7th century; design: uraeus-snake with the crown of Upper and Lower Egypt; Davies, no. 72)

In 2 Kings 25:25 and Jeremiah 41:1 an Elishama also appears, but further evidence to show that this is the same person is lacking.

Belonging to Jerachmeel, the son of the king.

(seal-impression; provenance unknown; 2nd half of 7th century; Davies, no. 508)

This Jerachmeel is probably identical with Jerachmeel, son of the king, who is mentioned in Jeremiah 36:26 as one of the courtiers who had to take Jeremiah into custody, after he had displeased Jehoiakim with his prophecies.

Belonging to Neria[h, the so]n of the king.

(seal-impression; provenance unknown; 7th century; Davies, no. 507)

The name Neriah is known as that of the father of Baruch and Seraiah, from whom (as we shall see shortly) seal-impressions have also been discovered. We have, however, no indication that he might have been a 'son of the king'.

The servant of the king

Just as 'minister' really means 'servant', so one could translate this title as 'slave of the king'. Yet it is the title of the highest functionary at court. As the king is called 'the servant of the Lord' to indicate that he rules in the name of God, so this 'prime minister' derives his power from the king and is called his 'servant'. The only 'servant of the king' who is mentioned in the Old Testament is called Asaiah (2 Kings 22:12, 2 Chronicles 34:20). Seals supplement this information, and from this it is evident that the title was also current outside Israel. It is necessary to distinguish two types: seals with the designation 'the servant of the king' and seals with the designation 'servant' followed by the name of the king. Since seals have also been discovered with 'servant of' and then a name which no Israelite king ever bore, it is necessary to reckon with the possibility that it is not the servant of a king who is involved here but one of an unknown person, who coincidentally bore the same name as one of the kings.

Belonging to Jaazaniah, the servant of the king.

(seal-stone; Tell en-Nasbeh; *c.* 600; design: cock in fighting pose; Davies, no. 69)

Fig. 16   Seal of Jaazaniah, the servant of the king

There is a tendency to identify this Jaazaniah with the Jaazaniah (2 Kings 25:23) or Jezaniah (Jeremiah 40:8) who was one of the followers of Gedaliah. It is in fact remarkable that the seal-stone was found at Tell en-Nasbeh, ancient Mizpah, because that is where Gedaliah and his supporters were killed. If we are indeed dealing with the same person, this seal-stone is the silent testimony to a drama which may be reckoned among the most gruesome passages in the book of Jeremiah (Jeremiah 41:1–19).

Belonging to Obadiah, the servant of the king.

(seal-stone; provenance unknown; 8th or 7th century; Davies, no. 70)

It has been thought that this Obadiah is the same as the person of this name who appears in 1 Kings 18:3, but given the dating of the seal-stone that is impossible,

Belonging to El(i)shama, the [se]rvant of the king.

(seal-impression; provenance unknown; 7th century; Davies, no. 504)

The only Elishama in the Bible who might possibly come into consideration for an identification with this one is the scribe Elishama mentioned in Jeremiah 36:12. If that is in fact the same person, he must then have won promotion, seeing that servant of the king was a higher office than scribe.

Belonging to Gedaliah, the servant of the king.

(seal-impression; provenance unknown; 7th century; Davies, no. 505)

There are various candidates for an identification. In the first place one can think of the royal steward Gedaliah, whose seal-impression was mentioned above. In addition there are two biblical characters with the same name who could come into the reckoning: the already-mentioned Babylonian governor Gedaliah, the son of Ahikam, and Gedaliah the son of Pashhur, an adversary of Jeremiah mentioned in Jeremiah 38:1.

> Belonging to Shema, the servant of Jeroboam.

(seal-stone; Tell el-Mutesellim; 8th century; design: roaring lion; Davies, no. 68)

The seal-stone was found at Tell el-Mutesellim (Megiddo) in 1904. It duly came into the hands of the Turkish sultan in Constantinople and later went missing there – the finest Hebrew seal-stone which was ever discovered! In view of the preciousness of the stone and the workmanship it can be supposed that we are in fact dealing here with a seal of a servant of the king. The king must then have been Jeroboam II (787–747) on account of the date of the seal. It

Fig. 17   Seal of Shema, the servant of Jeroboam

has been presumed that Shema had another seal made, as he would have lost his original one at Megiddo (it was evidently the fate of this seal to get lost). It is without doubt a fanciful story, for it would be a great coincidence if the seal-stone found in Jerusalem with the text 'Belonging to Shema, the servant of the king' (Davies, no. 71) were really the property of the same Shema.

> Belonging to Ashna, the servant of Ahaz.

(seal-stone; provenance unknown; 8th century; design: sun-disc with two uraeus-snakes; Davies, no. 141)

In view of the date 'Ahaz' may refer to the Judaean king of that name (735–715).

Belonging to Jehozarach, the son of Hilkiah, the servant of Hezekiah.

(seal-impression; vicinity of Hebron; end of the 8th century; Davies, no. 321)

This seal-impression has already been discussed above (see p. 75).

Belonging to Shebanyaw; (*reverse*) Belonging to Shebanyaw, the servant of Uzziyaw.

(seal; provenance unknown; 8th century; design on the obverse: man standing, with staff; reverse: two winged sun-discs; Davies, no. 67)

This richly decorated seal-stone could have belonged to a minister of the Judaean king Uzziah (783–742), in view of its date.

Manservant

Besides the Hebrew word *ʿebed* (translated in this book as 'servant') there is also the word *naʿar* (here rendered by 'manservant'). From the fact that a number of 'menservants' had their own seal at their disposal it may be deduced that some menservants had a position of some importance, for example as steward. In one such case it is conjectured that we are dealing with a manservant of a king:

Belonging to Eliakim, the manservant of Yochin.

(seal-impression; found at various places: Tell Beit Mirsim, Beth-shemesh and Ramat Rahel; date disputed; Davies, nos. 108, 277, 486)

The 'Yochin' would then be identical with the Judaean king Jehoiachin (597 B.C.E.). But is it likely that a manservant of a king who reigned for only three months under particularly unfavourable circumstances (see p. 116) had the opportunity to have a seal made? Moreover voices are now being raised in favour of dating this seal in the 8th century. With that this identification should be abandoned for good.

Scribe

In chapter 2 we have already spoken about the function of the 'scribe' as a royal official. The most famous of these scribes is undoubtedly Baruch, the faithful companion of the prophet Jeremiah and one of the authors of the book of Jeremiah. When the Israeli specialist in the field of seals Avigad one day got to hold a seal-impression of this Baruch in his hand, it quite took his breath away, as he was unable to avoid noting in his scholarly publication of this seal.

> Belonging to Berechiah, the son of Neriah, the scribe.

(seal-impression; provenance unknown; 7th century; Davies, no. 509)

Because of the precise combination of father's name, name of profession and date it is pretty well certain that this seal-impression was made with the seal of Jeremiah's secretary, who was evidently known officially as Berechiah. What a sensation it would have been if the papyrus on which this *bulla* (seal-impression) was fixed had also been discovered: an original document written by one of the authors of the Bible, even though it would probably have been a dull contract! But the fire which baked this *bulla*, so that it was preserved, simultaneously burnt up the papyrus.

Fig. 18   Seal-impression of Berechiah, the son of Neriah, the scribe

Probably the seal of Baruch's brother Seraiah, the son of Neriah, has also been found (Davies, no. 780). He was chief chamberlain to Zedekiah and accompanied the king to Babylon when he went for an audience with his overlord (Jeremiah 51:59). At Jeremiah's request he then pronounced a curse against Babylon which was recorded in writing by Jeremiah – remarkable behaviour for an envoy, but it demonstrates that he too must have been an adherent of Jeremiah, just like his brother Baruch.

Priest

Priests too could be appointed by the king and they too required seals for the administrative duties which they had to fulfil alongside their more priestly activities.

[Belonging to Za]karyaw, the priest of Dor.

(perforated seal; vicinity of Samaria; 8th century; Davies, no. 323)

This seal is also inscribed on both sides; on the other side stands: 'Belonging to Zadok, the son of Micah'. In view of the modest cost of this limestone seal-stone there must have been a special reason why someone had a second inscription executed on this stone. Possibly we are dealing with a son (Zakaryaw) who out of considerations of filial piety took over the seal of his father (Zadok) for fresh use. This seal is interesting for the fact that we now know that there must have been a YHWH-sanctuary in the coastal city of Dor – for nothing was known of a sanctuary there before.

Governor

From the Persian period seal-impressions are known belonging to the governor of Samaria and possibly also Judah. The latter is not certain, because some scholars want to read here not 'governor' but 'potter'. But the idea that these seal-impressions (Davies nos. 106:14–106:18) in fact derive from a potter does not seem very probable to me.

That the other bulla (Davies, no. 408) does indeed derive from Isaiah, the son of Sanballat, the governor of Samaria, is generally accepted. This bulla comes from the very important discovery of papyri and seal-impressions which was made in the Wadi ed-Daliyeh in 1962, but still has not been fully published! These are documents which possibly belonged to a group of Samaritans who were fleeing from Alexander the Great, a flight which they did not survive.

Doctor

In a group of fifty-one bullae which were found in 1982 during excavation of the remains of a house in Jerusalem from the late monarchy period there was sadly only one text with an indication of the owner's profession:

[Belonging to TBŠLM], the son of Zakkur, the healer.

(seal-impression; Jerusalem; c. 600; Davies, no. 804)

Another interesting feature of this group of bullae is the seal-impression of Gemariah, the son of Shaphan (Davies, no. 802), since a scribe of that name is mentioned four times in Jeremiah 36.

Seals belonging to women

Besides this group of seal-stones and impressions a second group have received particular attention, namely those belonging to women. We have here some interesting socio-economic source-material, which offers an important corrective to the picture which one gets from the Old Testament of the position of women in ancient Israel. There one gets the impression that women never or hardly ever took independent action in legal or financial affairs. Through the discovery of ten seals which belonged to women it is now an established fact that a number of women did without doubt know a certain economic independence, for otherwise they would not have had any need of these seals. On the seals they are mostly designated as 'the daughter of . . .' or as 'the wife of . . .'. Sometimes also by their own name alone, as on a richly decorated seal-stone from the 9th or 8th century which has the name Jezebel inscribed on the back (is this the wife of Ahab?).

In this connection mention should also be made of a beautiful seal from the 7th century with a picture of a lyre which belonged to 'Maadana, the daughter of the king' (Davies, no. 781). The most important of these seals comes from the Persian period. This is a seal-impression from the 5th century 'Belonging to Shelomit, the slave-girl of Elnathan, the governor'. Since it does not seem very likely that a slave-girl would have had a seal of her own at her disposal, this designation has been compared with the title 'servant of the king' and it has been presumed that here we are dealing with a female equivalent of this high official. If this interpretation is correct – it is disputed – then women too held political office in ancient Israel (at least in the Persian period). Already from the Old Testament we knew of the political role of the queen-mother, who had a special position, so this discovery is not a complete surprise, but more of an important addition to our knowledge of the socio-economic conditions in ancient Israel. The same can be said in general about the type of discovery which occupied the central place in this chapter. But however important this is, the most characteristic aspect of Israel is its religion. Hence the last chapter will be dedicated to the new information which inscriptions have provided in the area of the religious situation in ancient Israel.

Chapter 11

BLESSED IS URIAH:
TEXTUAL EVIDENCE OF ANCIENT
ISRAELITE RELIGION

The most characteristic feature of ancient Israelite culture is without doubt its religion, as we know it from the Old Testament and as it found its continuation in Judaism. The religious ideas of the writers of the Old Testament are so strongly distinctive in their character from those which we know from ancient Near Eastern literature, that the origin of Old Testament religion will probably always remain inexplicable from a scholarly standpoint.

Yet it is important to track down, as well as we can, the context within which this religion received its form, and in this inscriptions can be of great importance, as we have affirmed several times in this book already. The Mesha stele let us see how the Old Testament conception of God as the Lord of history developed from the conviction that the national god supports his or her people in battle and if he (or she) does not do so this is caused by divine anger, which must be propitiated.

The Deir 'Alla text strongly reminded us of the stories about the prophets in the Old Testament, while here also judgement prophecy had the aim of calling people to repentance. The role of belief in YHWH in daily life was clear from the Arad and Lachish ostraca. Whereas we should begin a letter with 'Dear Sir or Madam' and inquire after the health of the person concerned, these Judaeans expressed a wish for divine blessing: 'May YHWH let my lord hear tidings of peace and good fortune right now!' In the naming of a child, too, they remember the Lord, who caused the child to be born: very many Judaean names end in the theophoric element '-iah' (-*yahu*).

Despite the deep relationship with YHWH which emerges from these texts, religious practice in ancient Israel came under heavy criticism from the side of the prophets. They taught the people that YHWH cannot be worshipped alongside other deities. Anyone who serves other gods is false to God. In this connection they recalled a distant past when religion was supposed to have been pure.

In the period of the Babylonian exile the prophets went one step further. Up till now the prophets and their followers had not yet denied that the other gods really existed. These foreign gods did indeed exist, but they were fit only for the 'nations', the heathen who worshipped them in the form of images. Israelites, on the other hand, should only worship their own national god YHWH. The unknown prophet whom we call Deutero-Isaiah, who lived in the second half of the 6th century B.C.E., however, declared unambiguously that there is only one God, and that is YHWH:

> Thus says the LORD, the King of Israel
> and his Redeemer, the LORD of hosts:
> 'I am the first and I am the last;
> besides me there is no god.'   (Isaiah 44:6)

Monotheism had been born.

In the monarchy period the religious situation was still significantly different. Beside the group which was zealous for the worship of YHWH alone, the majority of Israelites saw no objection to combining the worship of the God of Israel with that of other gods or to using cultic objects in worship which aroused the loathing of the writing prophets, such as standing stones, sacred poles and even images. This was already known to us from the Old Testament, but quite recently discoveries of texts have been made which clearly underline this once again.

The inscriptions of Khirbet el-Qom

At Khirbet el-Qom, which lies 14 km west of Hebron, two tombs were discovered in 1967, in which inscriptions were encountered. The inscriptions in the first tomb are less interesting: they come from the end of the 8th century:

> Belonging to O[phai], *the son* of Netaniah.
> Belonging to Ophai, the son of Netaniah, is this (tomb-)chamber.

Both inscriptions thus have the same purpose, namely to indicate that in this tomb a certain Ophai has been laid to rest.

The third inscription, from about 750 B.C.E., which was

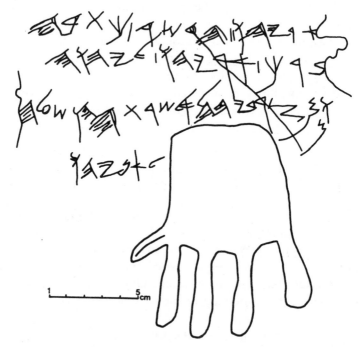

Fig. 19 Inscription from Tomb II at Khirbet el-Qom (from *ZDPV* 87 [1981], 140)

found in another tomb at Khirbet el-Qom, is much more interesting, though its interpretation is still disputed. The problem with this text is that the surface on which it was inscribed displays a large number of scratches, and the writer had great difficulty in carving the letters well. What did he intend to represent a letter and what is a scratch without any meaning? On this there is still no unanimity, but probably the following stands written there:

> Uriah, the *rich* (man), wrote it. Blessed is Uriah by YHWH – from his enemies he delivered him by his asherah. By Oniah. And by his asherah, his a[she]rah.

The function of the last two phrases within the whole is unclear. Do we have a second inscription here, which remained unfinished? Further, it is not certain whether Uriah refers to himself as 'the rich man', 'the governor' or 'the singer' – you can see that in Hebrew epigraphy there are many possibilities!

But the importance of this text lies in its central section. Uriah is blessed by YHWH, for he has delivered him from his enemies. Up to this point the text has nothing special: we meet such statements repeatedly in the Psalms. What sounds less biblical, however, is the addition of 'by his asherah'. It has been suggested that the meaning should be: 'Blessed is Uriah by YHWH and by his asherah – from his enemies he has delivered him'. But as the text now stands, YHWH's asherah is the means whereby he brought deliverance to Uriah.

What is an *asherah*? This Hebrew word is known from the Old Testament. Originally it was the name of a goddess, the wife of the Canaanite high god El, who is equated with YHWH in the Old Testament. In addition it can indicate a sacred tree or pole; this symbol for fertility and female sexuality was set up in the vicinity of an altar. In the Old Testament it is reckoned as a sign of idolatry and it is reported of both Hezekiah and Josiah that they had asherahs hewn down.

From the Khirbet el-Qom text, however, it appears that the asherah was not a foreign cultic object, but originally formed part of the worship of YHWH. The text speaks emphatically of '*his* asherah': the asherah belongs to YHWH himself and it is through his asherah that he brings about deliverance. This is very remarkable, for in the Old Testament YHWH is kept far apart from any fertility cult. Whereas the other deities of antiquity often prove themselves to be sexually active with one another, nothing of the kind is said of YHWH. In this text, however, he has a female fertility-symbol beside him, which is described as 'his'.

In this connection reference should also be made to the discovery of texts which was made opposite Aswan in Egypt, at ancient Elephantine, where a garrison of Jewish mercenaries was stationed. These texts are not dealt with separately in this book, because they were not found in the land of Israel itself, but they offer interesting information about the life of these Jewish colonists, who arrived there in the 7th or 6th century, though the texts themselves come from around 400 B.C.E. They are important from a religious point of view too, as it appears from them that a temple for YHWH (they, however, wrote YHW) existed at Elephantine. But these colonists seem to have worshipped other gods as well as YHWH, such as Anat-Bethel, Eshem-Bethel and Herem-Bethel. On one papyrus (from the end of the 5th century), for example, an account is given of silver that was collected for YHWH, but at the end it appears that only roughly a third was set apart for YHWH himself, with the rest going to Eshem-Bethel and Anat-Bethel. A clear indication that no sharp distinction was made between YHWH and the other gods – not even then.

To return for a moment to the Khirbet el-Qom inscription: with the text there is also a drawing of a hand (see Fig. 19). Is there a connection between this drawing and the special meaning which the Hebrew word for 'hand' (*yad*) can have of 'tomb monument' (cf. 2 Samuel 18:18 and Isaiah 56:6)? Or do we have here a hand which is to ward off danger, just as, still today, one may wear a 'hand' as an amulet?

Texts from Kuntillet ʿAjrud

Approximately 50 km south of Kadesh Barnea lie the ruins of Kuntillet ʿAjrud, where Israeli excavations took place in 1975 and 1976. A building was discovered there, which was interpreted by the excavator, Z. Meshel, as a religious centre for the use of people who travelled through this region with caravans and could here make their prayers and bring their gifts. Long ago the building ceased to serve its original purpose, after which this site remained otherwise unoccupied – a fortunate situation for the excavators. The building is dated to the end of the 9th century and the beginning of the 8th century B.C.E.

The ground-plan (Fig. 20) shows a special ancillary building (no. 1) which lies just to the east of the centre itself. Possibly the travellers were received here after their tiring journey through the desert. By way of a vestibule (no. 3), which was provided with benches, one entered immediately the most important room of the main building (no. 4). This room was also provided with benches, in this case on all sides. In addition, on the two short sides of the chamber store-rooms were built on. It looks as if people gathered in this room to worship the gods and to pray to them for a successful journey. The offerings which they had brought could be laid on the benches. After a while they were removed to the store-rooms on either side. According to the well-known French epigraphist A. Lemaire, however, this interpretation is incorrect: there was a schoolroom here, where people learned the art of

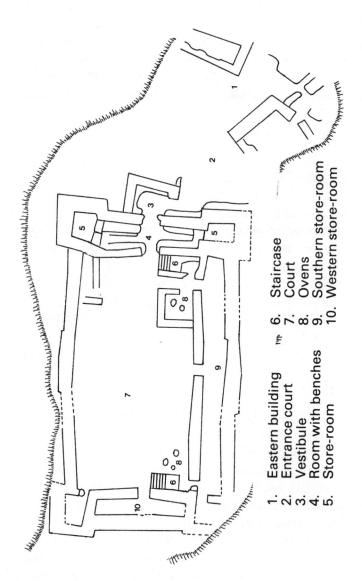

1. Eastern building
2. Entrance court
3. Vestibule
4. Room with benches
5. Store-room
6. Staircase
7. Court
8. Ovens
9. Southern store-room
10. Western store-room

Fig. 20 Ground-plan of the building at Kuntillet ʿAjrud.

the scribe. Now a school in the barren isolation of the desert would without doubt have been unusually well suited to form character, but it is not very practical. For this reason the interpretation as a religious centre seems more probable to me, if we are not dealing with a type of building like the later caravanserai.

In the middle of the building there was a wide open court, on to which the other rooms opened and which served for the storage and preparation of food. The walls of the most important rooms were covered with a layer of white plaster. On the plaster decorative motifs had been executed in some places, and in others texts were inscribed (see also chapter 6).

The texts on the plaster – five in number – are in poor condition. Three of them, written in black ink in the Phoenician alphabet, were found in the 'bench room' (no. 4). The first is no longer legible. As for the second, it is still discernible that it is a religious text, in which 'blessing' and 'good treatment' are spoken about. Both YHWH and his asherah are mentioned. It is not the only text from Kuntillet 'Ajrud where this combination appears, as we shall see below.

The third inscription derives from a different religious tradition:

. . .And in the way of El . . . Blessed (is) Baal on the day of . . .
The name of El on the day of . . .

El and Baal are the two dominant gods in the texts from Ugarit (see p. 10); possibly this was true for the whole Canaanite area. As already noted, in the Old Testament El is equated with YHWH. The Baal cult, on the other hand, was sharply repudiated. If we should be dealing here with an Israelite writer who used the Phoenician alphabet in place of the Hebrew, he belonged to the large group of Israelites who come in for strong criticism in the Old Testament.

By the entrance to the western store-room (no. 10) the

remains of two more inscriptions with a religious content were found. In them both YHWH and Baal are mentioned. What we are waiting for is the definitive edition of all these texts, so as to establish their precise character.

Some further texts have also been discovered. A number involve letters which were incised before firing on storage jars, like those which have been encountered elsewhere. Pottery has also been found on which a name, or the designation LŚRʿR (possibly 'belonging to the governor of the city' – see p. 140 – or alternatively a name), was incised after firing. In addition stone vessels have been found with inscriptions on them; the most interesting reads:

> Belonging to Obadyaw, the son of Adna. He is blessed by YHWH.

But the most important of these finds is a group of texts accompanied by drawings from around 750 B.C.E., which are inscribed on storage jars in red ink. The interpretation of the drawings (see Fig. 21) is in part still disputed, and we shall not

Fig. 21   Drawing on pottery from Kuntillet ʿAjrud

go into it here. The text of two of these inscriptions is given by Meshel in his preliminary excavation report (in fact an exhibition catalogue):

> Said E . . . the . . .: Say to Y . . . and Yoasah and [to X and Y]: I have blessed you by YHWH of *Samaria* and by his asherah!

The text is reminiscent of those from Khirbet el-Qom: YHWH and his asherah again stand side by side. But the distinctive feature of this text is that mention is not made of YHWH without further qualification, but of YHWH of Samaria. The latter phrase looks strange: Meshel still translated it 'who guards us', but that is less appropriate to the context. Such a linking of the name of a god and a geographical expression had already been known for a long time for other gods. Thus Baal Zaphon was worshipped alongside Baal-Zebul. Not that there would be any question of another god here, but Baal was worshipped in a particular manifestation, just as today Mary of Lourdes can be distinguished from Mary of Fatima without thereby intending to encourage the idea that there might be more than one Mary.

If the interpretation of this text from Kuntillet ʿAjrud given here is correct (in addition there is possibly, as we shall see below, a reference to YHWH of Teman, an epithet which recalls Habakkuk 3:3: 'God shall come from Teman'), we now know that YHWH also had various manifestations under which he could be worshipped. This casts new light on the name YHWH Sabaoth, whose interpretation is a matter of dispute. May we not be dealing here too with a special manifestation of YHWH, for example as he delivers Israel with the help of his heavenly hosts?

The second blessing may be translated as follows:

> Amaryaw said: Say to my lord, *Is it well*? I bless you by YHWH of Teman and by his asherah. May he bless you and may he keep you and may he be with my lo[rd] . . .

Again the combination 'YHWH and his asherah'. Who is meant by 'my lord' is not clear; certainly there is a striking parallel between the second part of this text and the priestly blessing in Numbers 6:24:

> May YHWH bless you and keep you . . .

A third blessing is no more fully preserved, but what remains of it can be translated as follows:

> [I bless you] by YHWH of Teman and by his asherah. All that he asks from . . .

Because of the lack of the conclusion it remains unclear who is the subject of 'he asks'.

From all this it will have become very clear that the study of the texts from Kuntillet 'Ajrud will be an important topic in future research on the history of ancient Israelite religion.

Silver amulets

During excavations at Ketef Hinnom by the Scottish Church in Jerusalem, which were under the direction of the Israeli archaeologist Gabriel Barkay, tomb-chambers were discovered, among other things, from the 7th and 6th centuries B.C.E. These were later severely damaged in the Byzantine period, when blocks of stone were hewn out from here for the construction of a church. But enough has survived for us to ascertain how these chambers must once have looked. By means of a door-opening and steps one entered the hewn tomb-chamber of some three by three metres. On three sides benches were left, sometimes provided with headrests. On these the mortal remains were laid, sometimes of several persons together on one bench.

It was the custom at that time, when the corpse had decomposed, to remove the bones and deposit them elsewhere. For this reason quite large repositories were hewn out under some of the benches, in which the bones could be kept. In this way a family could continue using the same tomb for centuries. The biblical expression, that someone 'was gathered to his fathers', is thus to be understood in its literal sense.

The gifts which had been presented to the deceased also eventually found their way into the repository. In most cases these cellars were emptied by robbers, but by a lucky chance one repository was found at Ketef Hinnom which had suffered no damage previously. In it were found the remains of at least 95 bodies, 263 pieces of pottery, jewels, forty arrowheads and countless other objects. From the nature of the finds it can be deduced that this tomb must have been in use for roughly six centuries.

Among these grave-gifts there were also two small scrolls of silver leaf which it was possible, with some difficulty, to unroll. On both of them a text could be seen to have been engraved. Because of the many wrinkles in the silver leaf the letters are very difficult to identify, but in view of their forms they most probably date from the 7th or 6th century B.C.E. Not much could be made out, until it was discovered that on both plaques a part of the text corresponded closely to the priestly blessing, already cited in part, from Numbers 6:24–26. It was a great sensation: it was even postulated that these little scrolls, which certainly did service as amulets, might be the oldest fragments of the Bible discovered till now.

This seems to me a premature conclusion. 'Fragments of the Bible' is in any case an unfortunate term. We are not dealing here with texts which contain exclusively passages from the Hebrew Bible. There are also other words there (till now only very partially deciphered), such as the name of the person for whom the amulet was probably intended. Therefore it might be more appropriate to speak of extracts from the Bible.

But even that seems to me not entirely precise. For the blessing on the amulets is noticeably shorter than the priestly blessing in Numbers, even though it is less terse again than the second blessing from Kuntillet ʿAjrud, which was translated above. Therefore these inscriptions are better regarded as forerunners of the priestly blessing which reached its definitive form in Numbers. If that is so, then this textual discovery makes clear once again how freely the biblical writers worked over existing texts before taking them over. They were no slaves of the tradition: the tradition inspired them precisely to find new forms and thoughts.

Sacred vessels

In preceding sections reference has already been made to letters which were inscribed on pottery before it was fired. A religious interpretation is often given to these letters. However, it seems to me that some reservations are required here. As soon as an archaeologist can no longer understand something, there is a strong tendency to interpret it in cultic terms.

It is of course very natural to do this with a krater from Beersheba, on which – here, however, after firing – the letters QDŠ are inscribed: this must indeed mean something like 'sacred' (date: 8th century). Possibly the contents of this krater were intended for the sanctuary, even though it was found in a private house. At Hazor too a bowl was found on which QDŠ was incised twice (date: 8th century). That may also be the meaning of the letters QŠ which were inscribed on two offering-bowls from the sanctuary at Arad (date disputed). There is also a third inscription from Arad (date not given) which certainly reads QDŠ.

A text on an ivory pomegranate

The same term QDŠ was also found on an ivory pommel in the form of a pomegranate which turned up in 1979 on the antiquities market in Jerusalem. The inscription is, however, more extensive; it can possibly be translated as follows:

> (Property) of the hou[se of YHW]H, sacred for (the) priests.

On the basis of the script this inscription is dated around 700 B.C.E., that is the time of king Hezekiah. Possibly this pommel adorned the sceptre of a high-ranking priest in the Jerusalem temple: the pomegranate is mentioned a number of times in the Old Testament as a decorative motif.

Inscription from a cave near En-Gedi

A very unusual text was discovered in 1974 in a cave near En-gedi. The text, from around 700 B.C.E., was written on a stalactite in black ink, a rather strange place to write an inscription. The cave is very difficult to reach: what can have been the reason for the writer to have taken his scribe's palette with him there? Was he a fugitive? Because of the rather unsuitable surface less than half the inscription remains legible today:

> Cursed be he who shall erase . . . Blessed is YHW[H] . . . Blessed (is he) among the *nati[ons]* as King. Blessed (is) my lord . . .

We are clearly dealing with a religious text here, written by a trained hand, in which YHWH is glorified. Had the writer perhaps had a mystical experience here which he wanted to record on the spot? We shall never know.

Gold from Ophir

At Tell Qasileh, an ancient harbour-town just to the north of
Tel Aviv, two ostraca were found in 1945 and 1946, which on
the basis of the script can be dated at the end of the 8th
century. The first concerns a delivery or a payment of taxes:

> For the king. *A thou[sand]* . . . oil and *a hundred* . . . Chiah.

The second inscription has been interpreted in a religious
sense:

> Gold from Ophir, for Beth-Horon. 30 sh(ekels).

For instead of reading Beth-Horon as a place-name it is also
possible to translate: 'the house of Horon', by which a
sanctuary of this Canaanite god would then be meant. This
however seems to be extremely improbable. It will be a
reference to a delivery of pure gold (Ophir-gold; cf. 1 Kings
9:28; 10:11) destined for the city of Beth-Horon.

A papyrus from the 7th century

There is another text for which a religious interpretation has
been proposed but where a more secular one is more likely.
This is a papyrus which was found in 1952 in a cave in Wadi
Murabbaʿat near the Dead Sea. Because of its great antiquity
(date around 650 B.C.E.) this is a unique discovery, since – as
we have already noted frequently with regret – texts on
papyrus do not have a long life-expectancy in the climate of
Israel. To date Papyrus Murabbaʿat 17 is the only papyrus
from the period before the exile to have been discovered.

Because papyrus was an expensive material, a sheet would
sometimes be used several times, the original text being
scraped off (*palimpsest*). That also happened to this sheet of
papyrus, but through modern technology it is possible to
make the first text visible again. The later text is less

interesting: four names with a number and an indication of a measure after them. Of the older text, however, more than half is still legible:

> Says ... -iah to you. [S]ent, yea I have sent peace (for) your house. And now, you should not listen to eve[ry] word that ... speaks to you ...

Although it has been proposed to interpret this text as a record of a prophecy, it seems more probable to me that we have a letter here: the sending of 'peace for your house' then means 'Greetings to your family'.

The confession of faith from Khirbet Beit Lei

As a conclusion to this book I have chosen a text which one could properly call a Judaean confession of faith. We are dealing here with graffiti which were discovered in 1961 on the walls of the main chamber belonging to a tomb in Khirbet Beit Lei, 8 km east of Lachish. Just as at Kuntillet 'Ajrud there is visible here a combination of drawings and texts, which were incised on the rock-wall. Besides two ships and circles three human figures were discovered. The first possibly has a lyre in his hand, the second stands praying, while the third has a strange object on his head. There has been a tendency to interpret these figures as Levites. We might have the tomb of a Levitical family here. This seems rather speculative to me, for what is the meaning of Levites with ships?

Because the writer probably had to do his work by the faint light of an oil-lamp and the surface of the rock-wall is covered with scratches (just as is the case at Khirbet el-Qom), it is difficult to determine what exactly is there. Even the dating is the subject of strenuous argument. The Persian period has been proposed, but also the time of Josiah, and even that of Hezekiah. The end of the monarchy seems most probable to me.

We shall discuss the three most important of the nine texts here; a possible translation of the first reads as follows:

> YHWH is the God of all the earth,
> The mountains of Judah (belong) to the God of Jerusalem.

The text consists of two lines of poetry. In the first the emphasis is laid on the universality of YHWH, in the second on the election of Judah and Jerusalem. The beginning of the text calls to mind Isaiah 54:5, in which Deutero-Isaiah calls the people to be no longer afraid, since the God of all the earth is Israel's saviour. Precisely in this universal aspect of YHWH there lies for Israel the basis for putting their confidence in him alone. It is possible that this idea is also involved in the first line here.

The expression 'the mountains (plural) of Judah' occurs only in 2 Chronicles 21:11. The normal practice is to speak of 'the cities of Judah' or 'the mountain (singular) of Judah'. In view of the place where this text was found, however, this designation is not surprising: Khirbet Beit Lei is in the hill-country of Judah. Even the region where the writer possibly sought for refuge, when an enemy had invaded Judah, belongs to YHWH and he can reckon on his help. The expression 'the God of Jerusalem' also occurs only in Chronicles (2 Chronicles 32:19), but the conviction that there is a close bond between YHWH and Jerusalem dates already from the monarchy period, and the parallel with Chronicles thus does not necessarily require us to locate the text in the same period as that book of the Bible (Persian period).

Two other texts are prayers to YHWH. The reading is again much disputed, as far as the first of these two is concerned:

> Care, *YHWH*, (in) *mercy*!
> Declare innocent, YH YHWH!

If that is the correct reading of this text, the writer calls God to take care of his people (cf. Psalm 80:14–15) and in his mercy to declare it innocent: the latter includes the idea that God should remit their punishment (cf. Psalm 19:13). As a context for this prayer a situation of military distress seems the most likely, for an invasion of the land by enemies was seen as a punishment from God (see p. 41). The third inscription confirms this interpretation:

Deliver, YHWH!

So in this tomb in the south of Judah a testimony has been found to the belief in YHWH as the deliverer of his people in times of distress. A Judaean who is otherwise unknown to us appealed to Him who is God of all the earth, but has willed to bind himself to Judah and Jerusalem. May he take care of the well-being of his people and be merciful to it.

BIBLIOGRAPHY

Works which are regularly cited elsewhere in this bibliography are followed by an abbreviation in bold type. After a general section the references are listed by chapter. For the academic journals the standard abbreviations are used.

General

Collections of texts in the original language with translations
G. I. Davies, *Ancient Hebrew Inscriptions: Corpus and Concordance* (no translations). Cambridge, 1991 (**AHI**)

D. Diringer, *Le iscrizioni antico-ebraiche palestinesi.* Florence, 1934 (**IAEP**)

H. Donner and W. Röllig, *Kanaanäische und aramäische Inschriften.* 3 parts. 2nd ed. Wiesbaden, 1966–1969 (**KAI**)

J. C. L. Gibson, *Textbook of Syrian Semitic Inscriptions. I. Hebrew and Moabite Inscriptions.* 2nd ed. Oxford, 1973 (**HMI**)

R. Hestrin et al., *Inscriptions Reveal: Documents from the time of the Bible, the Mishna and the Talmud.* Jerusalem, 1973 (**IR**)

K. Jaroš, *Hundert Inschriften aus Kanaan und Israel. Für den Hebräischunterricht bearbeitet.* Fribourg, 1982 (**HIKI**)

O. Kaiser et al., *Texte aus der Umwelt des alten Testaments* (twelve fascicles have been published so far). Gütersloh, 1982– (**TUAT**)

S. Moscati. *L'Epigrafia Ebraica Antica 1935–1950.* Rome, 1951 (**EEA**)

D. Pardee et al., *Handbook of Ancient Hebrew Letters.* Chico, 1982 (**HAHL**)

H. Reviv, *A Commentary on Selected Inscriptions from the Period of the Monarchy in Israel* (Heb.). Jerusalem, 1975 (**CSIPMI**)

Th. C. Vriezen and J.H. Hospers, *Palestine Inscriptions* (no translations). Leiden, 1951 (**PI**)

Collections of texts in translation alone

R. D. Barnett, *Illustrations of Old Testament History*. 2nd ed. London, 1977 (**IOTH**)

W. Beyerlin et al., *Religionsgeschichtliche Textbuch zum Alten Testament*. Göttingen, 1975 (**RTAT**) – Eng.tr. *Near Eastern Religious Texts relating to the Old Testament*. London, 1978 (**NERT**)

J. Briend and M.-J. Seux, *Textes du proche Orient ancien et histoire d'Israël*. Paris, 1977 (**TPO**)

K. Galling et al., *Textbuch zur Geschichte Israels*. 2nd ed. Tübingen, 1968 (**TGI**)

A. Jepsen et al., *Von Sinuhe bis Nebuchadnezar: Dokumente aus der Umwelt des Alten Testaments*. 2nd ed. Stuttgart etc., 1976 (**SN**)

A. Lemaire, *Inscriptions hébraiques. I. Les ostraca*. Paris, 1977 (**IH**)

H. Michaud, *Sur la pierre et l'argile: inscriptions hébraiques et Ancien Testament*. Neuchâtel, 1958 (**SPA**)

J. B. Pritchard et al., *Ancient Near Eastern Texts relating to the Old Testament*. 3rd ed. Princeton, 1969 (**ANET**)

E. J. Smit, 'Inskripsies uit Oud-Testamentiese Tyd', *Koers* 34 (1966), 55–78 (**IOTT**)

D. W. Thomas et al., *Documents from Old Testament Times*. 2nd ed. New York, 1961 (**DOTT**)

K. R. Veenhof, 'Nieuwe Palestijnse Inscripties', *Phoenix* 11 (1965), 243–260 (**NPI**)

Other general works

Y. Aharoni, *The Land of the Bible: A Historical Geography*. 2nd ed. London, 1979 (**LB**)

P.-E. Dion et al., 'Les types épistolaires hébréo-araméens jusqu'au temps de Bar-Kokhbah: Introduction', *RB* 86 (1979), 544–579

A. Lemaire, 'L'épigraphie paléo-hébraique et la Bible', *Supplement to Vetus Testamentum* 29 (1978), 165–176

E. Lipiński, 'North-West Semitic Inscriptions', *Orientalia Lovaniensia Periodica* 8 (1977), 81–117 (**NWSI**)

J. Naveh, 'Inscriptions of the Biblical Period', in H. Shanks and
B. Mazar (eds.), *Recent Archaeology in the Land of Israel*
(Washington and Jerusalem, 1984), 59–68

D. Pardee et al., 'An Overview of Ancient Hebrew Epistolo-
graphy', *JBL* 97 (1978), 321–346

G. B. Sarfatti, 'Hebrew Inscriptions of the First Temple Period –
a Survey and Some Linguistic Comments', *Maarav* 3 (1982),
55–83

J. Teixidor, 'Bulletin d'épigraphie sémitique' (survey of all new
discoveries; appears most years in *Syria* – note also the reprint
in a separate volume: *Bulletin d'épigraphie sémitique (1964–
1980)*. Paris, 1986)

Chapter 1 (selected references)

F. M. Cross, 'Newly Found Inscriptions in Old Canaanite and
Early Phoenician Scripts', *BASOR* 238 (1980), 1–20

J. Naveh, *Early History of the Alphabet: An Introduction to West
Semitic Epigraphy and Palaeography*. Jerusalem etc., 1982

K. R. Veenhof, 'Klei, kleitablett en spijkerschrift', *Phoenix* 24
(1978), 15–30

The Ahiram inscription:
ANET, 661; HIKI, 36–37; KAI II, 2–4; PI, 7–8; TGI, 49; TPO,
82; TUAT, II/4, 582.

J. C. L. Gibson, *Textbook of Syrian Semitic Inscriptions. III.
Phoenician Inscriptions*. Oxford, 1982, 12–17.

Chapter 2

General
HIKI, 34; IR, 9–13

A. Lemaire, 'A Schoolboy's Exercise on an Ostracon at Lachish',
Tel Aviv 3 (1976), 109–110

Idem, *Les écoles et la formation de la Bible dans l'ancien Israël*.
Fribourg etc., 1981

S. Warner, 'The Alphabet: an Innovation and its Diffusion', *VT*
30 (1980), 81–90

The 'Izbet Ṣarṭah Ostracon
AHI, 113; HIKI, 32–33
F. M. Cross, 'Newly Found Inscriptions in Old Canaanite and Early Phoenician Scripts', *BASOR* 238 (1980), 1–20 (esp. pp.8–15)
A. Demsky, 'A Proto-Canaanite Abecedary dating from the Period of the Judges and its Implications for the History of the Alphabet', *Tel Aviv* 4 (1977), 14–27
M. Kochavi, 'An Ostracon from the Period of the Judges from 'Izbet Ṣarṭah', *Tel Aviv* 4 (1977), 1–13
J. Naveh, 'Some Considerations on the Ostracon from 'Izbet Ṣarṭah', *IEJ* 28 (1978), 31–35

The Gezer calendar
AHI, 85; ANET, 320; DOTT, 201–203; EEA, 8–26; HIKI, 37–38; HMI, 1–4; IAEP, 1–20; IOTT, 56; IR, no. 8; KAI II, 181–182; NWSI, 82–85; PI, 12–14; SPA, 21–28; TUAT I/3, 247–248
H.-P. Müller, 'Notizen zu althebräischen Inschriften I', *UF* 2 (1970), 229–242 (esp. pp.229–231)
B. D. Rahtjen, 'A Note Concerning the Form of the Gezer Tablet', *PEQ* 93 (1961), 70–72
S. Talmon, 'The Gezer Calendar and the Seasonal Cycle of Ancient Canaan', *JAOS* 83 (1963), 177–187

Chapter 3

The Mesha stele
ANET, 320–321; CSIPMI, 9–34; DOTT, 195–199; HIKI, 41–50; HMI, 71–83; IOTT, 69–72; IR, no. 45; KAI II, 168–179; LB, 336–340; NWSI, 95–97; PI, 14–21; RTAT, 253–257 (NERT, 237–240); SN, 148–152; SPA, 29–45; TGI, 51; TPO, 90–92; TUAT I/6, 646–650
F. I. Andersen, 'Moabite Syntax', *Orientalia* 35 (1966), 81–120
P. Auffret, 'Essai sur la structure littéraire de la stèle de Mésha', *UF* 12 (1980), 109–124

J. Blau, 'Short Philological Notes on the Inscription of Mešaʿ', *Maarav* 2 (1979–1980), 143–157

A. Dearman (ed.), *Studies in the Mesha Inscription and Moab*. Atlanta, 1989

G. Garbini, *Storia e ideologia nell'Israele antico*. Brescia, 1986. Eng.tr. *History and Ideology in Ancient Israel*. London, 1988

C. H. J. de Geus, 'Koningsinscripties uit Moab uit de 9e eeuw v.Chr.', in K.R. Veenhof (ed.), *Schrijvend verleden: Documenten uit het Nabije Oosten vertaald en toegelicht*. Leiden etc., 1983, 25–31

A. Lemaire, 'Notes d'épigraphie nord-ouest sémitique', *Syria* 64 (1987), 205–216

E. Lipiński, 'Etymological and Exegetical Notes on the Mešaʿ Inscription', *Orientalia* 40 (1971), 325–340

J. Liver, 'The Wars of Mesha, King of Moab', *PEQ* 99 (1967), 14–31

J. M. Miller, 'The Moabite Stone as a Memorial Stele', *PEQ* 106 (1974), 9–18

P. D. Miller, 'A Note on the Mešaʿ Inscription', *Orientalia* 38 (1969), 461–464

W. Schottroff, 'Horonaim, Nimrim, Luhith und der Westrand des 'Landes Ataroth': Ein Beitrag zur historischen Topographie des Landes Moab', *ZDPV* 82 (1966), 163–208

S. Segert, 'Die Sprache der moabitischen Königsinschrift', *ArOr* 29 (1961), 197–267

K. A. D. Smelik, 'The literary structure of King Mesha's Inscription', *JSOT* 46 (1990), 21–30

R. Storr, *Die Unechtheit der Mesainschrift*. Tübingen, 1918

S. Timm, *Die Dynastie Omri*. Göttingen, 1982, 158–180

G. Wallis, 'Die vierzig Jahre der achten Zeile der Mesa-Inschrift', *ZDPV* 81 (1965), 180–186

Other Moabite Inscriptions – general
HMI, 83–84; IOTT, 72–73; NPI, 254–256; SPA, 43–45
C. H. J. de Geus, op. cit.

The second text from Dhiban
R. E. Murphy, 'A Fragment of an Early Moabite Inscription from Dibon', *BASOR* 125 (1952), 20–23

The text from Kerak
D. N. Freedman, 'A Second Mesha Inscription', *BASOR* 175 (1964), 50–51
W. L. Reed and F. V. Winnett, 'A Fragment of an Early Moabite Inscription from Kerak', *BASOR* 172 (1963), 1–9
G. Rendsburg, 'A Reconstruction of Moabite-Israelite History', *JANES* 13 (1981), 67–73
I. Schiffmann, 'Eine neue moabitische Inschrift aus Karcha', *ZAW* 80 (1964), 151–193 (esp. 169–172)
Idem, 'Archäologischer Jahrbericht', *ZDPV* 82 (1966), 274–330 (esp. 328–330)

Inscription from Samaria
AHI, 65; IR, no. 43

The Samaria ostraca
AHI, 39–57; ANET, 321; DOTT, 204–208; EEA, 27–39; HIKI, 51–57; HMI, 5–13; IAEP, 21–74; IH, 23–81, 245–250; IOTT, 56–57; IR, nos. 34–38, 41; KAI II, 183–186; LB, 356–368; NWSI, 85–86; PI, 21–27; SN, 161–163; SPA, 53–63
A. F. Rainey, 'The Samaria Ostraca in the Light of Fresh Evidence', *PEQ* 99 (1967), 32–41
Idem, 'Semantic Parallels to the Samaria Ostraca', *PEQ* 102 (1970), 45–51
G. A. Reisner et al., *Harvard Excavations at Samaria, 1908–1910*. I. Text. Cambridge, 1924, 227–246
W. H. Shea, 'The Date and Significance of the Samaria Ostraca', *IEJ* 9 (1959), 16–27
Y. Yadin, 'Recipients or Owners: A Note on the Samaria Ostraca', *IEJ* 9 (1959), 184–187

Chapter 5

Text on ivory plaque from Nimrud
AHI, 112; HMI, 19–20; NPI, 257–258; TUAT II/4, 564
A. R. Millard, 'Alphabetic Inscriptions on Ivories from Nimrud',
  Iraq 24 (1962), 41–51, esp. 45–49

Siloam tunnel inscription
AHI, 68; ANET, 321; CSIPMI, 35–40; DOTT, 209–211; EEA,
  40–43; HIKI, 71–72; HMI, 21–23; IAEP 81–102; IOTT, 57–
  58; IR, no. 75; KAI II, 186–188; NWSI, 87; PI, 28–29; SN,
  178–180; SPA, 64–72; TGI, 66–67; TPO, 117–118; TUAT
  II/4, 555–556
C. H. J. de Geus, *De Israëlitische stad*. Kampen, 1984, 82–94
K. M. Kenyon, *Jerusalem: Excavating 3000 Years of History*.
  London, 1967, 68–77
G. Levi della Vida, 'The Shiloah Inscription Reconsidered', in *In
  Memoriam Paul Kahle* (BZAW 103). Berlin, 1968, 162–166
H. Michaud, 'Un passage difficile dans l'inscription de Siloé', *VT*
  8 (1958), 297–302
H.-P. Müller, 'Notizen zu althebräischen Inschriften I', *UF* 2
  (1970), 229–242, esp. 232–234
E. Puech, 'L'inscription du Tunnel de Siloé', *RB* 81 (1974), 196–
  214
V. Sasson, 'The Siloam Tunnel Inscription', *PEQ* 114 (1982),
  111–117
N. Shaheen, 'The Siloam End of Hezekiah's Tunnel', *PEQ* 109
  (1977), 107–112
Idem, 'The Sinuous Shape of Hezekiah's Tunnel', *PEQ* 111
  (1979), 103–108
H. J. Stoebe, 'Ueberlegungen zur Siloahinschrift', *ZDPV* 71
  (1955), 124–140
Idem, 'Zu Vet. Test. VIII S.297ff. Henri Michaud, Un passage
  difficile dans l'inscription de Siloé', *VT* 9 (1959), 99–101;
  response of Michaud, *ibid.*, 205–209
Y. Yadin et al., *Jerusalem Revealed: Archaeology in the Holy
  City 1968–1974*. New Haven etc., 1976, esp. 75–78

Inscriptions on the rock tombs at Silwan
AHI, 73–74; CSIPMI, 41–45; HMI, 23–24; IAEP, 102–110; IOTH, 72–73; IOTT, 58–59; IR, no. 14; KAI II, 189; NPI, 244; NWSI, 87; SPA, 72–74; TGI, 65–66; TPO, 117; TUAT II/4, 558–559
N. Avigad, 'The Epitaph of a Royal Steward from Siloam Village', *IEJ* 3 (1953), 137–152
Idem, 'The Second Tomb-Inscription of the Royal Steward', *IEJ* 5 (1955), 163–166
H. J. Katzenstein, 'The Royal Steward (Asher ʿal ha-Bayith)', *IEJ* 10 (1960), 149–154
D. Ussishkin, 'On the Shorter Inscription from the "Tomb of the Royal Steward"', *BASOR* 196 (1969), 16–22
Idem, 'The Necropolis from the Time of the Kingdom of Judah at Silwan, Jerusalem', *BA* 33 (1970), 34–46

The Ophel ostracon
AHI, 65; EEA, 44–46; HIKI, 73; HMI, 25–26; IAEP, 74–79; IH, 239–244; IR, no. 138; KAI II, 188–189; NWSI, 87–88; RTAT, 268 (NERT, 252)

The Ophel inscription
AHI, 65
J. Naveh, 'A Fragment of an Ancient Hebrew Inscription from the Ophel', *IEJ* 32 (1982), 195–98
The other inscription is reported in Y. Shiloh & M. Kaplan, 'Digging in the City of David: Jerusalem's New Archaeological Project Yields First Season's Results', *BAR* 5 (1979) no. 4, 36–49, esp. 49

New Ophel ostraca
AHI, 65–66
A. Lemaire, 'Les ostraca paléo-hébreux des fouilles de l'Ophel', *Levant* 10 (1978), 156–161

The Qonerets inscription
AHI, 70
N. Avigad, 'Excavations in the Jewish Quarter of the Old City of Jerusalem, 1971 (Third Preliminary Report), *IEJ* 22 (1972), 195–196
Idem, *Discovering Jerusalem*. Oxford, 1984, 41

Tomb-inscription of Uzziah
HIKI, 104; IR, no. 255; PI, 39–40; TGI, 55; TUAT II/4, 576
J. A. Fitzmyer & D. J. Harrington, *A Manual of Palestinian Aramaic Texts*. Rome, 1978, 168–169, 223–224
J. Simons, *Jerusalem in the Old Testament: Researches and Theories*. Leiden, 1952, 206

Chapter 6

The text from Deir ʿAlla
TUAT II/1, 138–148
A. Caquot & A. Lemaire, 'Les textes araméens de Deir ʿAlla', *Syria* 54 (1977), 189–208
H. J. Franken, 'Nieuwe vondsten in Palestina: Problemen bij het opgraven van een tekst', *Natuur en Techniek* 35 (1976), no. 10
J. A. Hackett, *The Balaam Text from Deir ʿAlla* (Harvard Semitic Monographs 31), Chico, 1984
J. Hoftijzer, 'The Prophet Balaam in a 6th Century Aramaic Inscription', *BA* 39 (1976), 11–17
Idem, 'De Aramese teksten uit Deir ʿAlla', *Phoenix* 22 (1976), 84–91
J. Hoftijzer & G. van der Kooij, *Aramaic Texts from Deir ʿAlla*. Leiden, 1976
Idem (ed.), *The Balaam Text from Deir ʿAlla Re-Evaluated*. Leiden, 1991.
A. R. Millard, 'Epigraphic Notes, Aramaic and Hebrew', *PEQ* 110 (1978), 23–26, esp. 24–25
H.-P. Müller, 'Die aramäische Inschrift von Deir ʿAllā und die ältere Bileamsprüche', *ZAW* 94 (1982), 214–244
H. & M. Weippert, 'Die "Bileam"-Inschrift von Tell Dēr ʿAllā', *ZDPV* 98 (1982), 77–103

Ammonite inscriptions – general
W. E. Aufrecht, *A Corpus of Ammonite Inscriptions* (Ancient Near Eastern Texts and Studies, 4). Lewiston, etc., 1989.
L. G. Herr, 'The Formal Scripts of Iron Age Transjordan', *BASOR* 238 (1980), 21–34
K. P. Jackson, *The Ammonite Language of the Iron Age*. Chico, 1983

The Citadel inscription
F. M. Cross, 'Epigraphic Notes on the Ammān Citadel Inscription', *BASOR* 193 (1969), 13–19
W. J. Fulco, 'The ʿAmmān Citadel Inscription: A New Collation', *BASOR* 230 (1978), 39–43
S. H. Horn, 'The Ammān Citadel Inscription', *BASOR* 193 (1969), 2–13
E. Puech & A. Rofé, 'L'inscription de la citadelle d'Amman', *RB* 80 (1973), 531–546
W. H. Shea, 'Milkom as the Architect of Rabbath-Ammon's Natural Defences in the Amman Citadel Inscription', *PEQ* 111 (1979), 17–25
K. R. Veenhof, 'De Ammān Citadel Inscriptie', *Phoenix* 18 (1972), 170–179

The Tell Siran inscription
TPO, 141
G. W. Ahlström, 'The Tell Sīrān Bottle Inscription', *PEQ* 116 (1984), 12–15
B. Becking, 'Zur Interpretation der ammonitischen Inschrift vom Tell Siran', *BiOr* 38 (1981), 273–276
W. H. Shea, 'The Siran Inscription: Amminadab's Drinking Song', *PEQ* 110 (1978), 107–112
H. O. Thompson & F. Zayadine, 'The Works of Amminadab', *BA* 37 (1974), 13–19
K. R. Veenhof, 'Korte berichten: Een Ammonie(t)ische inscriptie', *Phoenix* 19 (1973), 299–301

Theatre Inscription
W. J. Fulco, 'The Amman Theater Inscription', *JNES* 38 (1979), 37–38

Chapter 7

AHI, 76–78; ANET, 568; CSIPMI, 46–55; HAHL, 15–24; HIKI, 76–78; HMI, 26–30; IH, 259–269; IOTT, 64–67; IR, no. 33; KAI II, 199–201; NPI, 248–251; TGI, 70–71; TPO, 134–135; TUAT I/3, 249–250

J. D. Amusin & M. L. Heltzer, 'The Inscription from Meṣad Ḥashavyahu: Complaint of a Reaper of the Seventh Century B.C.', *IEJ* 14 (1964), 148–157

Th. Booij, 'The Yavneh-Yam Ostracon and the Hebrew Consecutive Imperfect', *BiOr* 43 (1986), 642–647

F. M. Cross, 'Epigraphic Notes on Hebrew Documents of the Eighth–Sixth Centuries B.C.: II. The Murabbaʿat Papyrus and the Letter found near Yabneh-Yam', *BASOR* 165 (1962), 34–36

J. Naveh, 'A Hebrew Letter from the Seventh Century B.C.', *IEJ* 10 (1960), 129–139

Idem, 'More Hebrew Inscriptions from Meṣad Ḥashavyahu', *IEJ* 12 (1962), 27–32

Idem, 'Some Notes on the Reading of the Meṣad Ḥashavyahu Letter', *IEJ* 14 (1964), 158–159

Idem, 'Meṣad Ḥashavyahu', in *Encyclopedia of Archaeological Excavations in the Holy Land*, III, London, 1977, 862–863

D. Pardee, 'The Juridical Plea from Meṣad Ḥashavyahu (Yavneh-Yam): A New Philological Study', *Maarav* 1 (1978), 33–66

Idem, 'A Brief Note on Meṣad Ḥashavyahu Ostracon, 1.12: *wʾml*', *BASOR* 239 (1980), 47–48

V. Sasson, 'An Unrecognised Juridical Term in the Yabneh-Yam Lawsuit and in an Unnoticed Biblical Parallel', *BASOR* 232 (1978), 57–63

Idem, 'A Matter to be put right: The Yabneh-Yam Case Continued', *JNSL* 12 (1984), 115–120

Y. Suzuki, 'A Hebrew Ostracon from Meṣad Ḥashavyahu: A Form-Critical Reinvestigation', *AJBI* 3 (1982), 3–49

K. A. D. Smelik, 'De literaire structuur van het ostracon uit Javne Jam', in *Amsterdamse cahiers voor exegese en Bijbelse theologie* 7, Kampen, 1986, 114–122 (English summary on p. 144; an English version of this article will be published in *IEJ*)

Chapter 8

AHI, 11–38; ANET, 568–569; CSIPMI, 56–68; HAHL, 24–67; HIKI, 63–64, 75–76, 82–90; HMI, 49–54; IH, 147–235; IOTT, 67–69; IR, nos. 49–72, 137 and 166; LB, 399–400, 403–404; NWSI, 90–93, RTAT, 269 (NERT, 253); TPO, 141–142; TUAT, I/3, 251–252

Y. Aharoni, *Arad Inscriptions* (Judaean Desert Studies). Jerusalem, 1981

D. Conrad, 'On $z^e r \bar{o} a^c$ = "Forces, Troops, Army" in Biblical Hebrew', *Tel Aviv* 3 (1976), 111–119

H. Van Dyke Parunak, 'The Orthography of the Arad Ostraca', *BASOR* 230 (1978), 25–31

D. N. Freedman, 'The Orthography of the Arad Ostraca', *IEJ* 19 (1969), 52–56

V. Fritz, 'Arad in der biblischen Ueberlieferung und in der Liste Schoschenks I.', *ZDPV* 82 (1966), 331–342

Idem, 'Zur Erwähnung des Tempels in einem Ostracon von Arad', *Die Welt des Orients* 7 (1973–74), 137–140

C. H. J. de Geus, 'De opgravingen bij Tel Arad, Israel', *Phoenix* 18 (1972), 147–164

J. H. Hospers, 'Enkele oudhebreeuwse brieven uit Tel ʿArad, Israel (ca. 600 v.Chr.)', in K. R. Veenhof (ed.), *Schrijvend verleden: Documenten uit het Oude Nabije Oosten vertaald en toegelicht*, Leiden etc., 1983, 100–106

A. R. Millard, 'Epigraphic Notes, Aramaic and Hebrew', *PEQ* 110 (1978), 23–26, esp. 26

B. Otzen, 'Noch einmal das Wort TRKB auf einem Arad-Ostracon', *VT* 20 (1970), 239–242

D. Pardee, 'Letters from Tel Arad', *UF* 10 (1978), 289–336

A. F. Rainey, 'Three Additional Hebrew Ostraca from Tel Arad', *Tel Aviv* 4 (1977), 97–104

V. Sasson, 'The word TRKB in the Arad Ostracon', *VT* 30 (1980), 44–52

Idem, 'The meaning of *whsbt* in the Arad Inscription', *ZAW* 94 (1982), 105–111

M. Weippert, 'Zum Präskript der hebräischen Briefe von Arad', *VT* 25 (1975), 202–212

Y. Yadin, 'The Historical Significance of Inscription 88 from Arad: A Suggestion', *IEJ* 26 (1976), 9–14

Chapter 9

Ostraca from Lachish

AHI, 1–10; ANET, 321–322; CSIPMI, 69–93; DOTT, 212–217; HAHL, 67–114; HIKI, 91–95; HMI, 32–49; IH, 85–143; IOTH, 74–75; IOTT, 61–64; IR, nos. 77–78; KAI II, 189–199; NWSI, 88–90; PI, 30–35; SN, 197–199; SPA, 75–103; TGI, 75–78; TPO, 142–145; TUAT I/6, 620–624

N. R. Ganor, 'The Lachish Letters', *PEQ* 99 (1967), 74–77

C. H. J. de Geus, 'Lachis in Juda: Opgravingen en koningsstempels', *Phoenix* 26 (1980), 6–47

H.-P. Müller, 'Notizen zu althebräischen Inschriften I', *UF* 2 (1970), 229–242, esp. 234–242

A. F. Rainey, 'Watching out for the Signal Fires of Lachish', *PEQ* 119 (1987), 149–151

K. A. D. Smelik, 'The Riddle of Tobiah's Document: Difficulties in the Interpretation of Lachish III, 19–21', *PEQ* 122 (1990), 133–138

D. W. Thomas, 'Again "The Prophet" in the Lachish Ostraca', in *Von Ugarit nach Qumran* (BZAW 77), Berlin, 1958, 244–249

H. Torczyner, *Lachish I (The Lachish Letters)*, London, 1938

Y. Yadin, 'The Lachish Letters – Originals or Copies and Drafts?', in H. Shanks & B. Mazar (ed.), *Recent Archaeology in the Land of Israel*, Washington & Jerusalem, 1984, 179–186

The Adon letter
DOTT, 251–255; KAI II, 312–315; TPO, 135–136; TUAT I/6, 633–634
J. A. Fitzmyer, 'The Aramaic Letter of King Adon to the Egyptian Pharaoh', *Biblica* 46 (1965), 41–55
J. C. L. Gibson, *Textbook of Syrian Semitic Inscriptions II: Aramaic Inscriptions including Inscriptions in the dialect of Zenjirli*, Oxford, 1975, 110–116
W. H. Shea, 'Adon's Letter and the Babylonian Chronicle', *BASOR* 223 (1976), 61–64

Chapter 10

The Makbiram jar
AHI, 102; HIKI, 63–64; HMI, 18–19; IR, no. 111; NPI, 244; SPA, 49–52
J. Naveh, 'Belonging to Makbiram or "belonging to food-servers"', *EI* 15 (1981), 301–302

Inscribed jar-handles from Gibeon
AHI, 92–101; HIKI, 74–75; HMI, 54–56; IR, no. 106; NPI, 246–248; SPA, 110–112
N. Avigad, 'Some notes on the Hebrew Inscriptions from Gibeon' (Review Article), *IEJ* 9 (1959), 130–133
F. S. Frick, 'Another Inscribed Jar-Handle from El-Jib', *BASOR* 213 (1974), 46–48
J. B. Pritchard, *Hebrew Inscriptions and Stamps from Gibeon*, Philadelphia, 1959
Idem, 'More Inscribed Jar Handles from El-Jib', *BASOR* 160 (1960), 2–6

La-melek stamps
AHI, 246–249; IR, nos. 80–85; LB, 394–400; SPA, 112–114
D. Diringer, 'The Royal Jar-Handle Stamps', *BA* 12 (1949), 70–86
C. H. J. de Geus, 'Lachis in Juda: Opgravingen en konings-stempels', *Phoenix* 26 (1980), 6–47, esp. 31–45

P. W. Lapp, 'Late Royal Seals from Judah', *BASOR* 158 (1960), 11–22

A. Lemaire, 'Remarques sur la datation des estampilles "LMLK"', *VT* 25 (1975), 678–682

H. Mommsen, I. Perlman & J. Yellin, 'The Provenience of the *lmlk* jars', *IEJ* 34 (1984), 89–113

N. Na'aman, 'Sennacherib's Campaign to Judah and the Date of the *lmlk* Stamps', *VT* 29 (1979), 61–86

D. Ussishkin, 'Royal Judaean Storage Jars and Private Seal Impressions', *BASOR* 223 (1976), 1–13

Idem, 'The Destruction of Lachish by Sennacherib and the Dating of the Royal Judaean Storage Jars', *Tel Aviv* 4 (1977), 28–60

P. Welten, *Die Königs-Stempel: Ein Beitrag zur Militärpolitik Judas unter Hiskia und Josia*, Wiesbaden, 1969

Weights
AHI, 257–262; EEA, 99–105; DOTT, 227–230; HMI, 67–70; IAEP, 263–290; IR, nos. 91–98

Seals and seal-impressions
AHI, 118–246; DOTT, 218–226; EEA, 47–98; HIKI, passim; HMI, 59–64; IAEP, 111–261; IR, passim; PI, 35–38; SPA, 104–109; TUAT II/4, 565–572

N. Avigad, 'A Seal of "Manasseh Son of the King"', *IEJ* 13 (1963), 133–136

Idem, 'The Seal of Jezebel', *IEJ* 14 (1964), 274–276

Idem, 'New Names on Hebrew Seals' (Heb.), *EI* 12 (1975), 66–71

Idem, 'The Priest of Dor', *IEJ* 25 (1975), 101–105

Idem, *Bullae and Seals from a Post-exilic Judaean Archive*, Jerusalem, 1976

Idem, 'New Light on the Na'ar Seals', in *Magnalia Dei, The Mighty Acts of God: Essays on the Bible and Archaeology in Memory of G. Ernest Wright*, New York, 1976, 294–300

Idem, 'The Governor of the City', *IEJ* 26 (1976), 178–182

Idem, 'Baruch the Scribe and Jerahmeel the King's Son', *IEJ* 28 (1978), 52–56

Idem, 'The King's Daughter and the Lyre', *IEJ* 28 (1978), 146–151

Idem, 'The Chief and the Corvée', *IEJ* 30 (1980), 170–173

Idem, *Hebrew Bullae from the time of Jeremiah: Remnants of a Burnt Archive*, Jerusalem, 1986

Idem, 'A Note on an Impression from a Woman's Seal', *IEJ* 37 (1987), 18–19

G. Barkay, 'A Second Bulla of a *Sar Ha-ʿIr*' (Heb.), *Qadmoniot* 10 (1977), 69–71

R. Hestrin & M. Dayagi-Mendels, 'A Seal-Impression of a Servant of King Hezekiah', *IEJ* 24 (1974), 27–29

Idem, *Inscribed Seals: First Temple Period, Hebrew, Ammonite, Moabite, Phoenician and Aramaic. From the Collections of the Israel Museum and the Israel Department of Antiquities and Museums*, Jerusalem, 1979

Y. Shiloh, 'A Group of Hebrew Bullae from the City of David', *IEJ* 36 (1986), 16–38

F. Vattioni, 'I sigilli ebraici', *Biblica* 50 (1969), 357–388

F. Vattioni, 'I sigilli ebraici II', *Augustinianum* 11 (1971), 447–454

F. Vattioni, 'I sigilli ebraici III', *Annali del'Istituto Universitario Orientale di Napoli* 38 (1978), 227–254

K. R. Veenhof, 'Korte berichten: Het zegel van Baruch, zoon van Nerija, Jeremia's secretaris', *Phoenix* 24 (1978), 83–85

Chapter 11

W. A. Maier, III, *ʾAšerah: Extrabiblical Evidence*, Atlanta, 1986

J. H. Tigay, *You Shall Have No Other Gods. Israelite Religion in the Light of Hebrew Inscriptions*, Atlanta, 1986

Inscriptions from Khirbet el-Qom

AHI, 105–106; HIKI, 60–62; IR, nos. 139–141; TUAT II/4, 556–558

W. G. Dever, 'Iron Age Epigraphic Material from the Area of Khirbet el-Kôm', *HUCA* 40/41 (1969–1970), 139–204

G. Garbini, 'Su un'iscrizione ebraica de Khirbet el-Kom', *Annali del'Istituto Orientale di Napoli* 38 (1978), 191–193

J. M. Hadley, 'The Khirbet el-Qom Inscription', *VT* 37 (1987), 50–62

O. Keel (ed.), *Monotheismus im Alten Israel und seiner Umwelt*, Fribourg, 1980, 172–173

A. Lemaire, 'Les inscriptions de Khirbet el-Qôm et l'ashérah de YHWH', *RB* 84 (1977), 595–608

Idem, *Les écoles et la formation de la Bible dans l'ancien Israël*, Fribourg etc., 1981, 25–32

S. Mittmann, 'Die Grabinschrift des Sängers Uriahu', *ZDPV* 97 (1981), 139–152

M. O'Connor, 'The Poetic Inscription from Khirbet el-Qôm', *VT* 37 (1987), 224–230

Z. Zevit, 'The Khirbet el-Qôm Inscription mentioning a Goddess', *BASOR* 255 (1984), 39–47

Texts found at Kuntillet ʿAjrud

AHI, 78–82; HIKI, 58–59; TUAT II/4, 561–564

D. A. Chase, 'A Note on an Inscription from Kuntillet ʿAjrud', *BASOR* 246 (1982), 63–67

W. G. Dever, 'Asherah, Consort of Yahweh? New Evidence from Kuntillet ʿAjrud', *BASOR* 255 (1984), 21–37

J. A. Emerton, 'New Light on Israelite Religion: The Implications of the Inscriptions from Kuntillet ʿAjrud', *ZAW* 94 (1982), 2–20

J. M. Hadley, 'Some Drawings and Inscriptions on Two Pithoi from Kuntillet ʿAjrud', *VT* 37 (1987), 180–213

O. Keel (ed.), *Monotheismus im Alten Israel und seiner Umwelt*, Fribourg, 1980, 169–171

Z. Meshel, *Kuntillet ʿAjrud: A Religious Centre from the Time of the Judaean Monarchy on the Border of Sinai*, Jerusalem, 1978

Idem, 'Did Yahweh Have a Consort? The New Religious Inscriptions from the Sinai', *BAR* 5 (1979), no. 2, 24–35

Z. Meshel & C. Meyers, 'The Name of God in the Wilderness of Zin', *BA* 39 (1976), 6–10 [cf. also *BA* 40 (1977), plates A and B]
J. Naveh, 'Graffiti and Dedications', *BASOR* 235 (1979), 27–30

Silver amulets
AHI, 72–73
G. Barkay, *Ketef Hinnom: A Treasury Facing Jerusalem's Walls*, Jerusalem, 1986

Inscription on a krater from Beersheba
AHI, 75; HIKI, 58; IR, no. 73
Y. Aharoni, 'Chronique archéologique, Tel Beersheva', *RB* 78 (1971), 433–435, esp. 435
The inscription is illustrated in M. Avi-Yonah (ed.), *Encyclopaedia of Archaeological Excavations in the Holy Land*, I, London, 1975, 167

Bowl with inscriptions from Hazor
AHI, 104
The bowl is illustrated in Y. Yadin, *Hazor: The Rediscovery of a Great Citadel of the Bible*, London, 1975, 182

Offering bowls from Arad
AHI, 37; IR, no. 64
Y. Aharoni, *Arad Inscriptions*, Jerusalem, 1981, 115–118
F. M. Cross, 'Two Offering Dishes with Phoenician Inscriptions from the Sanctuary of 'Arad', *BASOR* 235 (1979), 75–78

Ivory pomegranate
AHI, 118
A. Lemaire, 'Une inscription paléohébraique sur grenade en ivoire', *RB* 88 (1981), 236–239

The Engedi inscription
AHI, 91–92; HIKI, 59–60; TUAT II/4, 561
P. Bar-Adon, 'An Early Hebrew Inscription in a Judean Desert Cave', *IEJ* 25 (1975), 226–232

The Tell Qasileh ostraca
AHI, 86; HIKI, 67–68; HMI, 15–17; IH, 251–258; IR, no. 42;
NPI, 244; NWSI, 86; SPA, 46–49

Papyrus Murabbaʿat 17
AHI, 111–112; HAHL, 120–122; HIKI, 73–74; HMI, 31–32; IR,
no. 32
P. Benoit et al., *Les Grottes de Murabbaʿât (Discoveries in the
Judaean Desert, 2)*, Oxford, 1961, 93–100
F. M. Cross, 'Epigraphic Notes on Hebrew Documents of the
Eighth–Sixth Centuries B.C.: II. The Murabbaʿat Papyrus
and the Letter found near Yabneh-Yam', *BASOR* 165 (1962),
34–46

The texts from Khirbet Beit Lei
AHI, 88–89; HIKI, 90–91; HMI, 57–58; IOTT, 59–61; IR, no.
79; NPI, 251–254; NWSI, 93–94; RTAT, 267–268 (NERT,
251); TUAT II/4, 559–560
F. M. Cross, 'The Cave Inscriptions from Khirbet Beit Lei', in
J. A. Sanders (ed.), *Near Eastern Archaeology in the
Twentieth Century: Essays in Honor of Nelson Glueck*, New
York, 1970, 299–306
A. Lemaire, 'Prières en temps de crise: les inscriptions de Khirbet
Beit Lei', *RB* 83 (1976), 558–568
P. D. Miller, Jr., 'Psalms and Inscriptions', *SVT* 32 (1981), 311–
332
J. Naveh, 'Old Hebrew Inscriptions in a Burial Cave', *IEJ* 13
(1963), 74–92
M. Weippert, 'Archäologischer Jahrbericht', *ZDPV* 80 (1964),
151–193, esp. 161–164

INDEX OF BIBLICAL REFERENCES

INDEX OF TEXTS DISCUSSED

(The texts are classified according to the place of their discovery)

CHRONOLOGICAL CHART

*c.*1200	Origin of Israel as a separate nation
	Saul
*c.*1000	David
	Solomon
	Gezer calendar
926	Division of the Kingdom

Israel		Judah	
926–907	Jeroboam I	926–910	Rehoboam
882–871	Omri		
871–852	Ahab		
852–851	Ahaziah		
851–845	Jehoram	868–847	Jehoshaphat
845–818	Jehu		
	Mesha stele		
	Samaria ostraca		
787–747	Jeroboam II	787–736	Azariah/Uzziah
	Amos		
	Balaam inscription	736–715	Ahaz
722/1	End of the Northern Kingdom		Isaiah
		715–697	Hezekiah
			Siloam inscription
		696–642	Manasseh
		639–609	Josiah
			Plea from Yavneh-Yam
			Jeremiah
		609	Jehoahaz
		608–598	Jehoiakim
			Ostraca from Arad
		597	Jehoiachin
		597–586	Zedekiah
			Ostraca from Lachish
		586	End of the Southern Kingdom
			Gedaliah